BOYS

An Anthology

Edited by
Zach Stafford and Nico Lang

A THOUGHT CATALOG ORIGINAL

Founded in 2010, THOUGHT CATALOG is owned and operated by The Thought & Expression LLC, an experimental media group based in Williamsburg, Brooklyn. THOUGHT CATALOG BOOKS is our book imprint, where we publish fiction and non-fiction from emerging and established writers across all genres.

Learn more about our organization and explore our library at thoughtcatalog.com/books.

Want us to publish your book? Email us the manuscript for review: manuscripts@thoughtcatalog.com.

Cover and interior design by Athletics NYC

THOUGHT
CATALOG
Books

ACKNOWLEDGEMENTS

THANK YOU TO MY mother for always supporting me, no matter what, and to my sister for being my biggest cheerleader. I would like to thank Chris for your supportive criticism and guidance over the years. 'Thank you' to all my friends and family who have asked me "How are you doing?" during the process of making this book and really meant it. Many thanks to my friend, comrade, roommate and non-licensed therapist Alex for living with me, for dealing with me, for never judging me and for listening to my daily rants. A special 'thank you' to Baldwin, to Didion, to Ellis, and especially to Junot Diaz who reminded me in 2012 that I do love stories more than anything in the world.

Finally, thank you to all the contributors in BOYS. Your stories, your lives, and your work have forever shaped me.

Zach Stafford

In their acknowledgements, most people thank those who have supported them along the way, the ones who fought for them and who were in their corner. Instead, I would like to thank the people who weren't, the ones who showed me why I should fight. To the kids in Middle School that threw my backpack in the garbage, who wouldn't let me sit with them on the bus and who reminded me again and again that I was the biggest loser in school, thank you for not making it easy for me. To the friends that laughed at me when you thought I wasn't listening, thank you for helping me realize I deserved better. To the teachers that made me feel different and weird, who reminded me that I didn't fit in, thank you for helping me stand out. To the boys that dumped me for not being enough, thank you for giving me something to write about.

To everyone who has ever told me I can't or I couldn't or I shouldn't or I won't ever or I'll never amount to, thanks for giving me someone to prove wrong.

Nico Lang

TABLE OF CONTENTS

FOREWORD

BOYS STARTED WITH WHAT seemed like a simple enough idea: We wanted to bring together gay men to tell their stories in a way that felt honest, personal and real. Our community is changing — generationally, technologically and geographically — as we continue to fight for our rights and grow as a community. How we document ourselves speaks volumes about our ability to know ourselves and write our own histories, and we need more opportunities to do that as our histories are unfolding. To know we are now is to begin to explore where we have been and to begin to reflect on where we are going.

However, the problem is that even asking an easy question isn't so easy. When we begin to ask where we are now and what our community really looks like, we must first address the way that community is represented — which is usually urban, middle-to-upper class and white. Saying the word "boy" in gay and queer male communities is constructed to mean a certain thing about what maleness is and isn't, who is included in our spaces and who is left out. You can tell a lot about a society by those they push to the margins, and our community doesn't leave much room for men of color, trans men, disabled men or anyone who doesn't look like our friends. We show them the door. We tell them they aren't allowed in here.

It's easy in our community to call for change from without — to demand that our politicians lobby for our civil liberties — but we believe that real change starts from within. We will never be one community, a monolithic dream under a united flag, and we don't seem to want to be. However, we can be communities that work together and advocate on each other's behalf, realizing that everyone's issues and stories have a right to be heard. Sometimes the most important changes aren't giant steps for mankind, but smaller ones — and sometimes it's not a step at all. It's simply sitting down at the same table with a willingness to hear perspectives that aren't your own and learn more about where are all coming from. Change is about learning to listen.

That's what BOYS is: It's about coming together not to speak but to listen and to learn about each other's histories. No one in this volume pretends to have an answer to the problems that face us, but we know where it starts. Change begins with an incitement to engagement and asking the questions we are often too afraid to. To quote The Real World, it's about when we stop being polite and start getting real. For us, realness was about representing our community as best as we could, highlighting issues of race, class, geography, economic background and gender identity, as a way of widening the space for discourse. We cannot fix the discussion, and our own scope is limited, but we can broaden it.

The stories included in BOYS range from hopeful and heartfelt to angry and critical — a diversity of styles, tones and themes as diverse as the community itself. For the volume, we asked each of the writers to give us a piece of their history — a part of them to put in a time capsule. Some of our authors wrote about the struggles of being transgender in a family that won't even recognize your chosen name and others wrote about what it's like to be able to be queer in your family — so long as you don't bring home a black man. It's about looking at the contradictions and the conflicts, moving from the sour to the sweet. Our hope is that by documenting our stories we can show that even at our darkest moments, we are not alone.

Our hope is that in sharing these histories, other publications, journals and outlets that focus on the gay male experience will begin to question the limiting ways that we are often portrayed, seeing not only the way others stereotype us but the ways by which we box in our own community. The goal is to show our readers that we are all so different, because we have all these disparate experiences, yet see the ways that our stories overlap, like a patchwork that just needs stitching. AIDS activists once put together a quilt to symbolically unite our struggles and find solace in death. With this volume, we want to make a blanket for life. It might not cover everything, but it will hopefully make us feel a little warmer.

1. VOMIT

JOE ERBENTRAUT | MADISON TO LOS ANGELES

IT WAS THREE DAYS after Christmas, 2004.

I was back home from my first semester at college and had been busy carb-loading and dancing gingerly around the fact that I was gay while catching up in conversation with my family.

Other topics I was actively avoiding: My partying at college, which had caused me to develop a bit of an absenteeism problem in several of my classes and to get my first-ever C in a non-math-related test; my first and fresh cartilage piercing, which I thought I was cleverly hiding by growing my hair long; and

1

my gaining at least 35 pounds from the aforementioned drinking and associated overeating.

But my new flab was the least of my worries. My first semester at University of Wisconsin had definitely had its ups and downs. Of course, I'd made some good friends — many of whom I still talk to almost a decade later — over the course of my adventures in borderline alcoholism. I also had achieved my inner emo kid's dream of becoming a professional t-shirt folder at Urban Outfitters, which was definitely going in the scrapbook.

But I had also started the semester out by being sexually assaulted and very probably drugged by an acquaintance I'd met over the Internet the previous summer.

I don't remember everything from that night, my first night out on campus, but I do remember drinking many glasses of a drink called a Tequila Moonrise and being slapped straight across the face and pushed out of a stranger's bed, while a crowd of people looked on, when I told my new friend I didn't want to have sex with him.

No, not the best start to my own personal "coming of (g)a(y)ge" story.

All of that packed into three months had left me feeling worn and my parents' overbearingness back home wasn't helping.

My dad is a staunch Reagan Republican with a penchant for all things Fox News, O'Reilly and Breitbart-approved. My mother doesn't much care for politics and generally, much like her son, preferred to avoid confrontation altogether. All that said, they were happy to have me home — so happy I couldn't go 10 minutes without some sort of a check-in.

My Livejournal commenters all agreed I was ripe for an escape and I heeded their advice. I would spend New Year's 2,000 miles away in southern California to not only see my ex-girlfriend for the first time since we broke up about one and a half years earlier, but also to meet her live-in girlfriend and my (for lack of a better term) new Internet crush.

Wait, how did that happen? Let me explain as best I can without the use of a diagram.

It was the early aughts and my family had just gotten The Internet. Dial-up, of course. Before long I was busily spending much of my free time writing on figure skating fan discussion boards — don't judge, I was hooked during the Nancy/Tonya scandal! — and talking to all sorts of strangers. Somewhere along the way, I met Izzy.

Izzy and I would spend long hours into the night chatting back and forth with each other first over ICQ, then Yahoo! Messenger and finally AIM. Before long, we discovered that, although she lived in southern California, she had close family ties to my humble corner of southeastern Wisconsin.

Eventually, we proclaimed ourselves boyfriend and girlfriend and the IMs graduated to multi-hour phone calls and the sort of handwritten letters that only teenagers who watched too many rom-coms at too young an age can write.

Just two years earlier, we met face to face for the first time when Izzy came to visit family in Wisconsin. We ate ice cream on the beach, we played miniature golf, and we went to the movies and cuddled close. We had an instant kinship, but despite our racing hormones, it never occurred to either of us to take off our clothes and take it from there every moment we had the chance. That probably should have been a sign.

By the spring of my junior year of high school, the week before our respective proms, I came out to her as being what I thought was bisexual at the time via an e-mail and she informed me that she identified the same way.

Izzy was brilliant, confident and beautiful in every way, with long straight hair that varied in shade from almost-black brown to bright fuchsia from month to month. Whereas she launched almost immediately from that point into a string of relationships with women, I was less successful in my attempts to date.

My first year and a half or so of dating consisted of secretive meetups with guys I met over XY.com, MySpace or HotOrNot.com. I sent photos of my erect dick to anyone and everyone who asked. I got in lots of cars with strangers and made out in lots of parking lots. Once I bought my "boyfriend" at the time a three-night stay at the cheapest motel in town and when I had to go in to work at the pizza restaurant where I waited tables, I kept him there *Misery*-style — just without any of the torture.

That motel is where I received my first-ever blow job.

*****

As I packed my bags for the trip the night before my flight, I felt a twinge of anxiety. Though Izzy and I had kept in touch, our friendship was definitely strained and there was no way to describe sleeping on the couch of your gay ex-girlfriend and her gay girlfriend for a week as anything but awkward. And I was also nervous to meet

Patrick — the aforementioned Internet crush — for the first time in real life.

Patrick was Izzy's only friend in high school who identified as both straight and male — until he came out as gay just six months before. At 19, he and I were the same age and Patrick had dishwater blond hair, a sturdy build and a biting sass to him. He worked in marketing like a real adult and had something I'd heard about in the movies called "a 401(k)."

In recent months, at Izzy's suggestions, we started spending long hours on AIM exchanging quips about the latest Tori Amos singles and our most recent dating failures. And we were both Scorpios which felt dangerous and exciting to me.

I'd long felt Izzy was trying to set us up, and I wasn't entirely opposed to that — even if I liked to play coy about it. For his part,

Patrick liked to fuck with me about whether he wanted to fuck me.

Jryan85:	what are you doing right now?
pstar117:	jerking off to those pics you sent ;)
Jryan85:	wait, really? what pictures are you talking about?
pstar117:	DUH! the ones i got from the secret camera i installed on your computer, slutballs
Jryan85:	…
Jryan85:	i've got to go. later, jerkface. xoxo

All of this was swirling through my mind as I stared into my closet, choosing armor for my adventure.

This was a situation that called for wearing black, all black, for the entire trip. Besides possibly concealing the weight gain, the goal was to broadcast an air of seriousness that somehow, all sexploits considered, I had it together. Isn't that why people vacation in the first place? So they can be a less polluted version of themselves even if it's just for a little while?

And I thought black-on-black-on-black would contrast nicely with my ghost-like Midwestern skin and the giant blue eyes that I inherited from my father, which friends and strangers alike regularly likened to an anime characters.

*****

My flight left at 9:05 a.m. on a Wednesday morning and my parents drove me to the Milwaukee airport to see me off. Seeing as my previous "Goth phase" had come to an end in seventh grade five years earlier, my Stevie Nicks-inspired attire probably tipped them off that something was up.

"You're the man in black, you know, Johnny Cash," my dad said to me as we hugged near the check-in counter. I could detect from a glimmer in his eye the hope that his gay son was on his way to somehow reconciling with his ex-girlfriend.

"Say hello to Izzy and you two have a wonderful time," my mother said, tears welling up in her eyes for a reason I, to this day, still haven't figured out. "Be safe, sweetie."

"Enjoy the land of fruits and nuts!" my dad said, cueing a well-deserved eye roll from both my mom and I.

About four hours later, I'd landed and was looking for Izzy, who was picking me up from LAX.

But I didn't see Izzy. First, next to her, my eyes fixated on a small, boyish person with large eyes, a giant forest green hoodie and baggy, wide-leg jeans. This was Paige, Izzy's girlfriend.

At 36 years of age, Paige was about 13 years older than Izzy and she had one of those large-gauge septum piercings that was always, endearingly, a little bit crooked. She looked like the coolest, cutest kid in my class — the coolest, cutest boy in my sixth-grade class, that is.

"You must be Joe!" Paige's embrace was warm and bright despite her cold, pale look and I immediately felt like an asshole for judging her. At this point in my overly sheltered life, I'd only met one other person who was even remotely androgynous in appearance.

"It's OK," Izzy said, as though she had read my mind and already accepted the silent apology. "Patrick's waiting in the car, are you hungry?"

We hopped in the car and that's when I met Patrick.

"Hey good lookin'," Patrick said as he helped me toss my duffle bag into the trunk. "Whatcha cookin'?"

He knew me too well. Food talk will get you everywhere with me.

"Hopefully something tasty! What's good in this city?"

Three hours later, after a weirdly tense falafel lunch, Izzy locking her keys in the car and a call to AAA, we had arrived at Izzy and Paige's apartment complex. We ascended the stairs to their unit, and as Paige went to unlock the front door, she found it was open. We were not alone.

"Put your keys in your knuckles," Paige instructed Izzy before she pulled a bottle of pepper spray out of her pocket and cautiously pushed the door open.

As we entered the apartment's living room, a white short-haired cat leapt at us from atop a bookcase and let out a loud yelp. The apartment was beginning to fill with smoke billowing from the general direction of the kitchen stove and the air smelled of burnt meat.

From the back bedroom, we heard a scream. And I was the only one alarmed at this scene.

"Fucking Puppy!" Paige yelled, before storming toward the bedroom. Izzy followed Paige and I followed Izzy.

Paige pushed the slightly-ajar door open and there lay a naked, long-haired man straddling an also-nude woman with curly mid-length black hair and heavy, heavy eye makeup.

"I told you, the next time you guys get stoned and fuck your brains out, wait to put the pizza in until after!" Paige said, exasperated, while the couple sat naked and bizarrely refrained from covering themselves up.

"Oh, Joe, these naked assholes are Puppy and Amber. Amber lives here with me and pays rent. Puppy lives here and doesn't."

*****

By the next afternoon, the smell of burnt pizza had finally dissipated. After the previous day's introductions, Izzy and I spent a low-key evening crying to Natalie Portman movies and talking about our respective college debuts. While Izzy kept directing the conversation toward my family, friends and forthcoming application to my school's journalism program, all I wanted to talk about was guys.

"I just don't get it. Madison was supposed to be this giant gay mecca and I already feel like I've met everyone there is to meet. It's so much easier for lesbians."

"You have no idea what you're talking about, Joe," Izzy replied. And she was right.

I was neurotic to the point of obsession, a color that looks good on exactly no one.

I spent the night trying to sleep on the couch, waking up about every half-hour or so to a raging war between the trio of cats who called the apartment their own personal battlefield.

At 5:30 a.m., for some reason, Patrick sent a text message I read in a half-awake state:

"i'm so glad you're here."

I still wasn't entirely sure if I was.

Early that morning, Paige and Amber both left for their 9-to-5s and Puppy left for — actually, no one had seen Puppy since I arrived yesterday afternoon but, again, this apparently wasn't unusual. But Izzy and I had breakfast of oatmeal, after which I promptly fell asleep again — for another eight hours.

When I opened my eyes, the coffee table in front of me was filled with many, many bottles of liquor and mixers and Patrick was ready with a camera.

"Smile, pretty, pretty princess!" Patrick said before snapping my photo. "It's New Year's Eve Eve. Are you ready to get fucked up?"

My ears perked up. Of course I was ready.

I took a shower and got dressed in the tightest black button-up dress shirt I'd packed. I put a thin layer of body glitter on my arms and a thick line of black eyeliner on my upper lids. I was determined to have sex that night and I was convinced the body glitter was going to help set those wheels into motion.

I also wore the lone pair of "sexy" underwear I had packed in my duffle: a black pleather and mesh thong with a metal zipper in the front.

I said it was "sexy," not classy.

We hopped in a car, all the booze piled into a box the size of a mid-90s desktop computer, and made our way to the party.

When we arrived at the modern, well-decorated apartment for the party, a ladies-on-ladies episode of Real Sex was on the TV, Frou Frou was blaring from the sound system and the lighting was dim and moody.

Once the bar was set up, Paige — who had taken on the role of bartender for the party — handed me a bright green drink.

"This is made special for you. Drink up."

And that I did. Over the next few hours, everyone at the party did. We danced, took shots and hugged repeatedly like the happiest of drunks. At one point, Patrick and I sat, just short of cuddling, close to each other on a couch. Someone asked if we were dating and Patrick replied, "It's complicated."

Later he asked, "Where do you see yourself in 10 years?"

"I don't know. Maybe with you?"

We both burst out laughing.

"You know, I just really hope I'm happy," I continued, between slurps of what must have been my seventh appletini.

"What if I was the one making you happy?"

"That could be all right," I giggled back at him with a giggle I'd never heard from myself ever before.

And then we kissed. I think.

The next thing I remember is dry heaving on the floor of the bathroom, peering through blurred vision at a toilet full of what looked like lime green Jell-O mix before it becomes Jell-O mixed with cat food. My throat burned and teeth hurt from the vomiting. My knees and arms were bruised, my fingernails were dirty.

The pounding on the door and shouts from the hall sounded something like a "Homogenic"-era Bjork song. I slowly pulled myself up to my feet and took a look in the mirror. My eyes were red from crying, my eyeliner had mostly relocated to my nose and the body glitter had somehow transferred to my mouth. I looked like a gay disco zombie.

At that moment, Patrick somehow broke his way into the bathroom and pulled me to the balcony to "get some air." And then I tried to make out with him. I unbuckled my belt and began to zip down my pants and let the "sexy" thong take the wheel. When he pushed me away, it was everything and it was nothing. I had never felt more alone.

"There's something here, right? But what do we do with that? Does it even matter if I want you?"

I was verging on screaming and I'm sure everyone at the party could hear me.

"Joe, I don't think you know what you want," Patrick told me. I knew he was right. "Come on. Let's smoke these cloves."

I smoked at least a half-dozen of those and eventually collapsed into a king bed shared by Patrick and at least three other people, all of them sprawled-out strangers.

I woke up and the first thing I saw was Patrick next to me. He awoke when I sat up, my head throbbing. For whatever reason, I couldn't help but stare at him.

"Don't worry, we didn't," Patrick whispered in my ear.

I didn't know whether to be disappointed or relieved. In so many ways, I still don't.

*****

The following night was New Year's Eve. As I watched Patrick make out with someone else at the San Diego house party, I felt a hot rage bubbling inside of me like a science-fair volcano.

I was ready to explode and that was OK.

"How are you doing?" Izzy asked, sliding in next to me, wearing a '20s-inspired shimmering cocktail dress in black. It didn't take long for her eyes to follow mine, darting toward the make out sesh-in-progress, while "Maps" by the Yeah Yeah Yeahs played over the apartment stereo — the best make-out song ever.

"I've been better, I guess I just sort of feel silly. Like everything with him I imagined and I'm just waking up."

I stared into my drink like I was waiting for it to grow eyes and stare back at me.

"Are you sure that's it though? I know he still cares a lot about you. I do too, for the record. Sometimes it's better when it's not meant to be."

When we hugged, I remembered the first time we ever hugged, two years before, in the parking lot outside a Walgreen's. So much had changed in those two years this touch, as it was bound to, felt different. It felt fuller and warmer.

At that moment Paige butted in with champagne glasses while the countdown to midnight began.

5! 4! 3! 2! 1!

I watched as everyone in sight rung in 2005 with a kiss, as you do. Patrick and his someone else kissed then disappeared out of the room into the night.

Izzy kissed me on the tear that had welled up on my cheek.

"I'll be OK."

"Of course you will. You don't have a choice. Happy New Year, dear."

*****

Two days later, I felt like I'd aged five years in one plane ride.

When "Maps" came on the mix CD Patrick had made me a few months earlier, it felt like my stomach dipped into my socks.

Back in Wisconsin, I felt shattered and vulnerable but also fully present for the first time since the assault I still couldn't call an assault. I felt like my skin was mine, all mine once again. When I looked in the mirror, I saw a person I didn't immediately want to turn away from. And I felt like I needed to dye my hair black.

Hair dyed the darkest shade of black I could get my hands on, I returned to school.

My second day back on campus, I received a letter from Patrick.

I don't remember what the letter said, but I think he apologized, which he didn't need to do. And he also wrote something along the lines of "I don't think we'll ever be what we both wanted, but we're going to keep on wanting. That's how we'll know we're alive."

I ripped the letter up, threw it in the trash and immediately wished I hadn't. That night, I dyed my hair brown again and then sat down at my laptop, opening up AIM for the first time in a week. When I saw Patrick sign in a minute later, I went to message him and instantly froze when "pstar117 is typing." flashed on my screen.

pstar117: hey boobear, how was your flight?
Jryan85:   oh, fine!
pstar117: good!

Five minutes — or whatever the length of Fiona Apple's "Paper Bag" is — passed.

Jryan85:   well, i've got to go.

pstar117:   <3

pstar117 has signed off.

2. A TRIP DOWN ROUTE 666

ERIC BELLIS | DOVE CREEK, COLORADO

THE WORST THING MY mother's ever done is kidnapping me when I was 19. That sounds really dramatic, doesn't it? It feels really weird to say. Who kidnaps their legally adult child? *My* mother. What made it even worse was that she took me because she was hoping she could find a way to pray away my gay. We haven't spoken in so many years that it hurts to count them, as if I were numbering her sins.

The story starts like this: I'm 19, living on my own, and employed as a barista at a busy coffee shop in the Old Market in Omaha,

Nebraska. I loved my life, I loved my new cool friends, and I loved not living with my parents. I was really happy. I lived in a huge house — a triplex, actually — with six, seven or maybe even eight other people. Rent was cheap. We partied all the time. I had a fake ID. I had a cool loft bed. I didn't have a girlfriend, but I had some crushes. This was a few years before I transitioned to being male so I was visibly queer, and the best thing was that in my new environment, I was allowed to be so.

My mother bluntly asked me if I was a lesbian when I was barely 15, then she forced me to break up with my girlfriend of nine months, even threatening to call the police. When I was 18, I was asked not to come back home a couple days after I graduated high school, all for refusing to remove a necklace covered in rainbow beads. The threat was probably idle, but I obliged. My mother told everybody that I ran away. When I was thirteen my stepfather told me I should commit suicide. This was before they even knew I was queer.

Though my mom and stepfather met at a metaphysical store and taught me to do Tarot and cast runes by the time I was nine, they found Jesus a few years later and turned into worse people than they already were. Jesus didn't want me to be gay, so for years it was just never discussed and I lived in shame and I was very, very, very depressed.

When I was 19, I thought I had a perfect life. Then my mother and stepfather decided they were going to move for the 89,773,827,432th time. My mother asked if I would come along and help out with driving. Even though my mother had hurt me and rejected me countless times, I said yes because

I love her and I was a lot sweeter and more helpful (read: naïve, overly-trusting and stupid) back when I was 19. I packed a bag and brought my boom box that had detachable speakers and my CD book. I wasn't quite sure how long I would be staying. I thought maybe two weeks at the most. My mother had promised she'd pay for a bus ticket or an airplane ticket home after they were settled in. And then the week turned into weeks, and the weeks into months. Two of them.

According to the 2009 U.S Census, Dove Creek, Colorado is a town with a population of 689 people. Its nickname is "The Pinto Bean Capital of the World." It is hot and dry, located in the Four Corners area. That is where they took me, along with my little brother and sister. At the time my mother may have been pregnant with my youngest sister whom I've only met a few times, back when she was an infant. The actual town was about five miles, give or take, from the ranch my mother and stepfather had rented. The closest town that had more than 689 residents in it was Cortez. It boasted a small downtown shopping area full of antique and cowboy kitsch stores. It was about 35 miles away from Dove Creek, which were both located off of what was then called Highway 666 (it is now called U.S. Route 491).

The drive out there from Omaha wasn't terrible. We took the scenic routes. It was actually kind of fun while I was still unaware of my mother's intentions to keep me there. We made pit stops and drove through mountain passages, and I got to drive the U-Haul part of the time. We snacked on beef jerky and fast food, and I almost forgot during the trip out there how screwed up things actually were. It was easy to pretend that we were a "normal" family (which I've since realized do not exist) and that they weren't running from Omaha because they probably fucked somebody over; their main source of income came in by conning people in fake business arrangements.

As time progressed and I realized that they weren't going to send me back to Omaha anytime soon, I tried to enjoy my stay on that rustic ranch while secretly plotting a way out. I fed the chickens (which are disgusting, filthy, and loud creatures) and helped my stepfather build an electric fence to keep the horses in and the coyotes out. I touched the fence every chance I got because I have a weird thing for getting shocked. I spent hours explaining my problems to the wise goats in our charge on the property, saved a hummingbird that was injured and quickly went through the meager bag of ditch weed I'd brought with me — smoking it in the barn while my mom thought I was shooting hoops. (I don't "shoot hoops.") We somehow acquired a bunch of kittens. I watched my little brother proudly help with chores on the ranch. He was so cute.

We had family excursions sometimes. We saw Anasazi ruins at Mesa Verde National Park in Cortez. We went to the Four Corners and I got to be in four states at the same time. We'd go to the tiny ice cream and burger joint in town and sit in the desert sun drinking milkshakes and eating cheeseburgers. One of my favorite things to do was to go to the feed store in town and look at all the tools and smell the different barrels of grains. We liked to go on drives and explore the Southwestern terrain. Even though I hadn't come out as trans yet, I was perfecting the art of passing as male, and out there in the rural southwest I usually passed to strangers, much to my mother's chagrin.

At night I would drink my mother's box wine, which always seemed to mysteriously be full, and go online and talk to my friends back home. I'd sleep until noon and wake up with a hangover. That was when I started drinking seriously, and it fucked me up in a major way. Looking back, I have a hunch that the wine was there and that 19-year-old me was allowed to go to town on it in "secret" because it kept me somewhat placated.

During those nights drinking wine, I was also trying to make arrangements to get back home. Friends offered to come and get me or send me money to get a bus ticket. When I sheepishly brought these options up to my parents, having figured out that their intention was for me to continue to live with them, my ideas were shot down. The internet history and my chat histories were searched. After that, I was banned from the internet. I still stealthily logged on at night, making sure to erase my history, and I managed to start building a plan that included my biological father, whom I'd only met the year before, driving out from his home in Iowa to come get me. It took a while to figure out logistics and to carry it out. In the meantime, things were getting really bad between my parents and me. The fights were getting worse and worse, I was sinking into a deep depression, the night drinking was getting intense, and I felt hopeless. I couldn't do anything without my parents. I didn't have any friends there and then my mother started suggesting I get a job in town and stay with them indefinitely.

As our fights escalated, I ran out of the house one day. It seemed random to my mother, but I had been planning it for a week, after getting an email through to my father without my mother's detection. In the message, my father told me to start a fight, let things get really bad and then storm out to go for a walk. I headed south on Highway 141 and then east on U.S. Route 491 (666, back then) to walk the five miles or so to the actual town of Dove Creek. I was probably about two miles into my journey, in the glaring sun, walking on an interstate that had heavy freighter truck traffic with barely a shoulder to walk on. The town sheriff, who would prove to be very helpful, stopped on the side of the interstate to ask me what I was doing out there, chastising me about the danger of walking on that particular interstate.

We'd met him several times. We were the new family in a town that didn't get many new families. He'd driven out to the ranch to welcome us personally. I was scared, and I didn't want to tell him that I was walking into town to find a payphone from which to call my father. I'd stolen quarters from my mother's wallet to pay for the long-distance call, and my father was waiting at home that day, all day, for my call. Dad and I were setting up a time for him to drive out and a day to try to come get me. Something was off about my story, and I could tell he knew that, but the Sheriff drove me into town and waited for me to use the phone. Then he drove me back home but respected my request that he drop me off a half-mile away on Highway 141 so that my family didn't see me coming home in a Sheriff's car. I would be forever grateful for this man.

The call set our plan in motion. I was to stage another argument the coming Sunday, and in the meantime, my father left Iowa that night and started his drive to Dove Creek. He got a hotel room and waited. And I waited, my stomach nervous all week, knowing that after this things would never, ever be the same. My ear ached knowing I was abandoning my siblings; without my presence they'd never have a link to anything close normalcy.

Sunday came around. As my orchestrated fight progressed and I refused to go to church with them, my mother gave in and let me stay home out of her own exasperation. After making reservations the day of the phone call, my father had emailed me the details that night when my parents had gone to bed. So that Sunday, I called him from their home phone, hurriedly packed my duffle bag and left my boom box with a note on it, saying that it was for my brother and that I loved him. I left another letter for the rest of the family explaining that I was okay and that I couldn't stay there.

I waited for my father to pull into the driveway. My stomach felt sick. I was afraid he wasn't going to show up, or that he would show up when they were coming home. I anticipated the worst.

My father had gone straight to the sheriff as soon as he got into town, unbeknownst to me. He told him the whole story, and the sheriff agreed to accompany him out to the ranch to pick me up. I panicked when I saw the sheriff's car, thinking that I was in trouble and that I'd somehow been tricked, but when he got out of the car and saw me he hugged me. He said he thought that there was something peculiar about my family since he first met us and that his suspicions were confirmed when he picked me up on the side of the interstate that day. Anticipating my parents possibly freaking out, he had decided that he would wait for them to return home from church to explain where I had gone, and to let them know that there was nothing they could do since legally, I was an adult.

It was over. And we left.

We headed straight back to Iowa. It was an adventure, and I was saved. My dad and I bonded during the trip back to the Midwest because up until that point, we had only known each other for a year. We were still basically strangers. When we got back to Iowa where we stayed for about a week with his mother, I decompressed and worked on getting my job back at the coffee shop in Omaha. I started putting my life back together after it had belonged to someone else for two months. While in transit, my mother called and left threatening messages on my dad's answering machine, and when my grandmother attempted to reason with her over the phone, she accused my father of kidnapping me himself. She said that I was a runaway. Threatening legal action because they were "harboring" me, she blamed her actions on my "lifestyle." She said that being gay wasn't the real me.

Slowly I have recovered from the experience, and I even visited my family for Christmas one last time. I went with my maternal grandmother (to protect me from another kidnapping), and my friends were aware of their new address in Oklahoma in case I turned up missing again.

That was a few years after the kidnapping — and right before I decided to transition. Once I came out as male, our relationship was over. I eventually stopped trying to get her to love me. I still ache for that love, but as I've gotten older, I've realized that she doesn't really know how to love if the given affection doesn't benefit her directly — meaning that she doesn't really know how to love at all. I found out later from my maternal grandmother (who is totally accepting of me as a trans man, as is the rest of my extended family) that my mother had planned to take me to an Evangelist church to have hands laid upon me, a grip she never wanted to let go. She thought that after years of me being queer that she and her nutty friends would be able to rid me of whatever demon it was that was making me that way. Yes, she thinks I am possessed. She also thinks she's a prophet, too, so there's that.

That was 13 years ago. I'm no longer a lonely teenager trying to escape a family that hurts them. I'm 32 now and still scared and still trying to escape the things that hurt me, but at least I'm in control of my life and I am safe and okay. I'm still working on the healing, and I will be for the rest of my life. And I know that I'm never going to feel as happy and as whole as I did when I was first out on my own, before Dove Creek, but I am free at least.

3. CONFESSIONS OF A SNOW QUEEN

ALOK VAID-MENON | BANGALORE, INDIA

THIS IS THE STORY of Brown. How it travels over state lines, oceans, and lips to feel beautiful. This is the story of beautiful — of learning the parts of us that cling on too hard for us to scratch them out, of the failure of human heart to desire more boldly. This is the story of a brown too bold to be beautiful, or too beautiful to be brown, or, in other words, a boy who no longer tries to use English to tell his story. This is their story.

My senior year of college I had enough. I took off the Fall semester from school and moved to Bangalore, India to organize with the queer Indian movement (read: find myself). Let's call it a naïve desi romanticizing the homeland. Let's call it a cliché. Let's call it foolish notions of finding Love and finding Brown and not being able to tell the difference.

*****

College Station

The story begins something like this. At the peak of its empire they say that the British controlled almost 85% of the world's landmass. India was the crown jewel — that place of tea, and mystique, but mostly sex. Colonialism they tell us was a project of benevolence. The civilized white people of the world were there to help us — we the brown, the abject, the queer. When they came to our lands, they talked about how sensual our women were, how our beauty was not gendered, the familiarity of our bodies with one another and the intimacy of it all. They brought words like "sin" and "homosexual" to describe the rhythms of our people, stifling our songs with sodomy laws and penal codes; they wanted to make us more pure for God and for profit. (Is there a difference?) And at some point, we began to believe them. We stopped speaking about sex, we ignored the thousand-year old-temples with gods of all genders fucking, and we threw the hijras on the streets and on our backs in secret. The Brits blew us so hard that we scattered like dandelion seeds across the world — English branded on our tongue, white branded on our heart.

My parents somehow landed in Texas. When you fly into the two-plane airport of College Station, the first thing you'll see is a sign that says: "Home of the George Bush Library." I was in elementary school when they opened the behemoth — that destination of every fourth grade field trip and that thing that finally put us on the map. That year, my teacher asked me to come to school wearing "traditional" clothes. When they would ask me who my favorite President was, I'd always say George Bush; he was the man who not only led the country when I was born, but held me — and the rest of the world — in his lap. There is a photo somewhere out there on the Internet that will prove it.

History repeats itself. When you exit the airport, go down Highway 6, turn onto Rock Prairie Road, and then I'll meet you at Arroyo Court — that house where Google Images first taught me the word "gay" (read: white). Then I'll take you down the road to my elementary school where I grew up developing crushes on white men with names and politics much like George. I'll show you the rooms where I used to write love letters to the white boys in my classes and sign them "from Crystal," hope that the swirl in the "L" would give me away — like the way I smiled too hard while we played truth or dare. This is the park, this is the school, this is the street, this is the town where I grew up loving white men and hating myself. This is where I grew up wanting to sleep with the very men who called me faggot, called me terrorist and noticed me.

It took me years to come out not because I was afraid, but because I didn't want my family to know that I was becoming white.

Growing up in Texas, I developed a bad case of white fetish. I could show you the porn I used to jack off to, and I could show the boys I fell in love with. I could tell you how the only representations of homosexuality I consumed were white, but in some ways that's only part of the story. You see, white fetish is a condition that's only partially about sex. For Indians white fetish is in our blood. It's why we moved to America, it's why we work hard to get in the best schools, it's why we buy skin lightening cream to feel beautiful. White fetish is ancestral violence inscribed in our bodies; it's a condition that describes the ways in which we are ready to be penetrated by America. Give us your racism, give us your Orientalist media representation, give us anything, and we will say thank you and keep quiet. We will check you in your hotel rooms, and we will hand you your groceries, and we will be your second-in command, and we will dress our kids in J. Crew and make them only speak English so we can be like you. And sometimes we think you believe us.

Pack all of your bags as fast as possible, dash back to that small goddamn airport and catch the first flight out to Houston, then connect to San Francisco, then run to

Stanford University and I'll show you the classrooms where I learned fancy words like "decolonize," the poorly lit dorm rooms where I shed tears and cloths and cum and tried to do it by letting white men inside of me when they told me they were "different from the rest." I'll introduce you to the first boys of color I met — the ones who called me beautiful but I didn't believe them because they did not have names like George.

So I told my parents I wanted to go back to India for a while. My Mom didn't get it, "Why would you want to go back?" I didn't really have the words for it at the time, but I felt the tug. I bought a ticket across the ocean and ran.

*****

Bangalore

Bengaluru Airport is nothing like College Station's. Outside there are a couple of fast food restaurants that all mean "food poisoning" when translated into English. Swarms of men smelling of that combination of sandalwood soap and sweat will ask you if you need a taxi. Push past the chaos with your luggage, button down shirt, and slacks. Your accent will mean that they will rip you off, undoubtedly, but they will listen.

The taxi will take you through the outskirts. Marvel at the billboards with faces that look like yours and gawk at the Ganesha at the mantle, the foreign made familiar. When the driver asks you where you are going, show him that chit of paper to your uncle's place near Abbas Ali Road, shukria. Move out as fast as possible. Find your own place. Oops, that bougie apartment in Vasant Nagar where there's even an interracial white/African couple and their boisterous child — complete with a gym! Do not tell your friends how much you are paying; remind all of your Skype calls back home that the currency rate is in your favor. Breathe in the salt, the sweat, the indigestion of India. Make home out of the leftovers Padma the cook leaves for you, that stray puppy you *picked up from the street, and the contemporary art you plaster all the walls. Do not think twice before you cross the road, just leap out. The eighteen lanes of traffic will mold around you. This is India.*

To get to work, tell the auto driver to take you to Infantry Wedding Hall. Dismount and walk across the street to what looks like abandoned house. This is actually your office. Push through the screen door (but make sure the kittens, puppies, and occasionally street children run out) and set your stuff down wherever you see a spot. Don't bother to open your laptop: your boss will ask you if you want a cup of chai. Do not say no even if you don't; they will think that you are rude as fuck. The trick is in changing the hand that holds the piping hot glass as frequently as possible in order to avoid burning yourself. Do not wince or seem disconcerted. Smile and sip as frantically as you can.

Before they ask me my politics, they ask if I have a boyfriend. The question arrives in different ways, always subtle. "So, are you single?" he asks, his eyes staring intently ahead as he negotiates all the traffic. It appears that the entire gay movement in India is polyamorous — finding ways to politicize their voracious libidos — so I try my best to fit in. I wear Bata chappals and over-compensate for the skinny chinos with an eager bobbling head and pseudo-accent (with a hint of cardamom). "Well, it's complicated…I'm not really interested in physicality…I'm more invested in the idea of…romantic friendships…building affective solidarity?" "Does that mean you are single?" "No, no, I'm not, but I'm not sure if I'm necessarily looking, either." I play my cards cautiously in this place where veins run slower than telephone lines, and secrets function as currency.

Another asks me as I cling on to him as he speeds his motorcycle down MG Road.

Maybe it is something about the wind on my face, the Bollywood drama and desperation or the accidental intimacy of the embrace, but I feel more at ease this time. "Do you have a boyfriend?" "No." "Why not?" "Umm...I don't know...I just..." My voice is lost in the sound of traffic.

Another asks me out for dinner at a cheesy American-themed restaurant. (Drunk is a language that transcends borders.) He is surprised that I don't fuck as much as him, "But we're young, you know. It's in our hormones!" So I try my best to tell him about racism in America — how white gays either ignore or fetishize us. I tell him about the first white boy I kissed — the one who told me that he always wanted to "be with a brown man because it makes him feel like he's with a real man." He nods his head in agreement but I think these are the lessons one has to learn in the flesh — seeing oneself as a Brown does not happen in India.

Oppression does not happen to me in India. I can't claim any political marginalization: me, the upper-caste, upper-class, English-speaking, male-passing buffoon who stumbles across the streets lost late at night — always safe. In fact, I am learning what it must feel like to be a white man in the U.S.: the whole world bending itself backwards for me. The auto drivers always stop when I wave my hand, the waiters trip over themselves to lay the napkin on my lap, and the men, well, the men all want to fuck me.

I realize this first when I walk into a local support group for queer men. There are about twenty-five of us in attendance. I am trying my best to keep calm as I join a circle of men who look just like the family friends I grew up with. We go around and introduce ourselves.

All eyes turn to me. "Hi, I'm Alok. I'm visiting from America." Their faces lighten up like diyas on Diwali. "Tell us more."

I join them for dinner after. They are joking about me in Kannada, Hindi, Tamil, all the languages we are losing across the ocean. "We should hang out. What's your number? Do you need a ride home?" Five of them escort me out to make sure I don't get ripped off from the auto driver. My phone is buzzing all night with texts: "Hey." "Wuts up?" " ;)" (The language of horniness transcends borders.)

It happens again the next week when I am volunteering to teach English to a group of kothi sex workers. I start first with the ABCs and one of them blurts: "U is for underwear! Do you wear boxers or briefs?" They ask for my number, if I want a massage, where I live, what it's like to live in America, fuck me

America. Two can play this game: "A is for Anus, B is for Buttocks, C is for Cock." They promise me they will come back next week.

That Friday I somehow direct the auto driver to this bar on the outskirts of Bangalore. Tonight there is some cheesy gay party my friends all tell me I must go to — with some theme like James Bond or AmericaTM. It is packed to the brim. Boys of all shades, smells, castes, regions and languages are actually dancing to the hybrid Bollywood/American fusion music. In the office we like to call the repeal of Section 377 — the British imposed sodomy law — the party law because all that can change is that gay men can now congregate in public. The city of Bangalore usually shuts down all parties by 11:00 (because late night dancing encourages prostitution). But for some reason, the gay parties keep booming until at least 1:00.

Everyone wants to know who I am. Everyone wants to dance with me. I have never felt more wanted and more desired in my entire life. And I know it's because my skin is lighter than theirs and I know it's because my passport is more American than theirs, but for a moment I feel beautiful and I want to believe that there is something in that. But then I notice the entire crowd stop moving. They are still dancing, but their eyes are turned to the entrance. Three white guys walk in and the entire pulse of the party changes. I notice the way we all continue taking to one another — but still glance back. I notice the way I feel that warmth in my body. I hate them so much, but I want to fuck them. We hate them so much, and that's why we want to fuck them. I go home early.

My colleagues accuse me of having a bad case of diasporic angst. "America is so hard, why don't you just move back here?" And it seems so simple, so doable for me, the foreign-educated rich Indian with U.S. dollars stuffed in his back pocket, the one who gets away with the nose piercing because the wealthy are excused from custom, excused from gender. And at first the prospect of it all seems so tantalizing: the food and the hospitality. But the white fetish is not gone.

Race finds a way to haunt me here. At the first queer youth social I attend, they berate me with questions: "Have you slept with a Latino before? I heard they have big dicks." "How do you know?" "I saw it on porn." "Have you slept with a white boy before? I heard they are cleaner than Indian men — more loving, more compassionate, more open, more tolerant, more accepting..." At the support group everyone talks about their dream of getting married: of having some white Fulbright scholar find them on Planet Romeo (Indian Grindr) and take them back to America. Leading gay activists aren't excluded from this: "Americans just have...a better sense of culture."

And I try my best to dull at the noise but at the end of the day I still believe them. I believe them as I use my high-speed Internet to watch Western porn of white men fucking each other. I believe them as I close the pop-up windows of Indian men — the first time I have ever seen bodies as hairy, as Brown as me on a screen. I believe them as I stumble on ex-pat parties with white boys at hotels that won't let in my friends and hate the American boy who dresses up as a "Mexican" for the Halloween party but still wants to take him home.

So my roommate makes fun of me for it: *Why haven't you brought a single boy back with you after all the parties you go to?* I don't have the language for it: the way the nice boy after the support group offers me a ride home on his motorcycle, the way the wind kisses our faces, the way he stops half-way and asks me for a drink and the way I sit on the steps of the road and I lie to him that I have a boyfriend. How to explain to a body that it is Brown? How to explain white fetish in a country which has been fucked for years? To a city whose most famous landmarks are the cum stains left from the British? To a city with a commercial street where you can buy Adidas sneakers and watch Hollywood movies in 3D.

Pick up an auto from Mantri Mall and ask it to drive you to the Design School outside of Bangalore. Meet up with your friends at the liquor store and sneak the girls into the house. Sit in the corner as your friends dance to the Bollywood tunes your hips cannot comprehend. Pretend to act drunk, even though you are not drinking. When the bottle spins to your direction, lean across the circle. Do not think about it: kiss him as they gasp and clap. Wake up the next morning and realize that this is the first Brown boy you have ever kissed.

Fly back home via London. Heathrow Airport is much larger than College Station's. Take the Tube all the way to his arms. Wait for him in the coffee shop in Queen's Lane. Open your eyes and pretend that you do not see him like the way you have hidden that photo of you and George Bush. Pretend that he is just the Skype screen. Pretend that he is just the friend. Pretend that he is just the past.

Fuck him that night. Wake up and recognize that he is white. That you are Brown. That nothing has changed.

4. MY CLOSET IS BETTER THAN YOURS

JOEY ALBANESE | NEW ORLEANS, LOUISIANA

WHEN I WAS IN the second grade, our entire school voted on which color the new M&M should be. We gathered in the tiny gym and formed groups based off of our color preference: blue, purple, or another color I can't remember. Almost the entire school formed a mass around the teacher holding a poster with a blue circle on it, and I huddled around the five other kids who chose purple. I didn't really like purple that much. Heck, I really didn't even like M&M's. But I wanted to be different. No, I knew that I was different, and I wanted everyone else to know that, but I couldn't. So too. My brother was on the blue side.

I never really had that rebellious stage that kids have growing up when they dye their hair pink, listen to music with offensive lyrics and wear whatever clothes in their closet that their parents disapprove of most. I was raised in a small town in Northern New Jersey with parents who never punished us; they simply had expectations, and if they were not met, a look on their faces was enough. As a result, I wanted to be everything my parents wanted me to be. I wanted to show them that I was special. I wanted them to be proud. And I never wanted to see that look on their face.

One of my earliest memories is when my brother and I would go over to our neighbor's house and play dress up. We'd put on his sisters' ridiculous costume dresses and shake around fake wands, prancing through the house like little fairies. One night after a day of these charades, my father asked me what we did at Scott's house earlier. I told him we played dress up, but when he asked what kind of dress up, I froze and told him "like Peter Pan." I couldn't tell him the truth. I didn't want to see that look on his face.

One night a little while after, I couldn't stand the guilt and woke up just to tell him the truth. Dad found me before I could even make it all the way down the stairs; parents have a funny way of doing that. "We really dressed up like fairies that one day, not like Peter Pan," I blurted out. He smiled and nodded his head, "Go back to bed."

The older I got, the more I felt like I was clinging to this Peter Pan costume. I would sit in bed and contemplate being truthful to my parents about this person I thought I was, but I couldn't. So instead I would just lie there and cry in my pillow as the dishonesty towards my family (and myself) continued to eat me alive. And when I would come up for air, I would look over at my brother sleeping soundly on the other side of the room, and wonder why I felt so different from this spitting image of me.

*****

I had no idea who I was growing up, and ironically, no one else did either. I grew up with an identical twin brother, and it wasn't until we were 18 that we found out we were both gay.

When people ask me how it was growing up with a twin, I don't really know what to tell them. I mean, I spent my entire youth getting mistaken for someone else by friends, teachers, even family members. To this day, our grandmother gets our names wrong more times than not. It was always a game for people to guess who was who. And we would just stand there, with fake smiles on our faces, forcing half-laughs out of our mouths, secretly offended that our lack of individual identity could be so entertaining for others.

Our identity was one. We were the twins. The boys. A group. An entity. A thing. It was, therefore, a constant struggle to separate myself from this false sense of self that I was born into due to everyone's instinct to group us together. We had the same cute bowl haircut that was so "in" in the early 90s. We would dress in the same outfits (him in the blue version, me in the red). We would often say the same thing at the same time in the same voice with the same intonation.

As kids, we both loved being in plays, even though we weren't very good. And for some reason, that was where I found solace. I loved the thrill of feeling like a unique individual. Someone whose life had some sort of specific purpose, even if that purpose was compressed into three short lines. I didn't care. Without those lines, the show just wouldn't be the same. And that made my adrenaline flow.

But there was also comfort in playing a predetermined part whose words were chosen, dances choreographed and costumes designed, all for him. It gave me the opportunity to surrender my insecure identity and become a face in a classic show like *Guys and Dolls* or *The Pajama Game*.

An actor. That was the first thing I wanted to be when I was old enough to formulate a well-informed opinion on the subject before I was corrupted by societal conditioning. I would sit for hours and hours, face to face with the television, obsessed with the complex lives of different characters and envious of their stories, their romances, all of it. It felt like a reality out of my reach.

It was around this time that I began having a reoccurring dream that has haunted me until recently. It's one of those typical dreams — the one where you're about to go on stage and realize you forgot to memorize your lines. The entire dream takes place before the show and involves me running around backstage with anxiety about how I'm not ready to go on. And I never am. Not once has a dream ever lasted long enough for the curtain to rise.

I've always been fascinated by the way our minds retain certain memories from our childhood with such vividness. There's a reason we hold on to them and struggle to make sense of it all. Probably because they hold truth about ourselves that are hard to understand at the time, so we subconsciously carry them with us until we do. And our minds create these anxiety dreams to help us figure it out.

One year in elementary school, in that same tiny gym that made me feel so small, our class put on a reenactment of "The Sorcerer's Apprentice," a segment in the Disney film, *Fantasia.* There were two sets of twins in our class, and it made sense that either they or we would play the dual lead roles: Real Mickey and Dream Mickey. My brother and I were chosen.

Dream Mickey had quite the epic scene where he moves oceans and controls the galaxy, yet it lasted all but one minute in the 10-minute short. So when the teacher asked me to play that part, it didn't feel so epic. I played the shadow role, one that I continued to play for most of my childhood.

My personal identity was constantly threatened by daily comparison: who did better on an exam, who didn't strike out at a baseball game and which looked better in their class photo that year. Growing up for me became one big petty fight to stay above water.

He would one-up me in almost every aspect of our childhood: he was in a more advanced math class than I was, he became the president of our class (until high school graduation), and in the eighth grade, he received an outrageous award for being the "most outstanding citizen."

The thing is, I didn't really care about any of that stuff, yet it meant the world to me. Because even though I thought I knew who I was, no one else did. Or at least it felt that way. If you're not careful, others' perception of you starts becoming your own. And that's how I got lost.

In high school, I began making decisions either because they were the opposite of my brother's or to avoid seeing that look on my parents' faces. I took Wood Shop instead of Art. I chose to become a lifeguard instead of a camp counselor. I became captain of the track team instead of joining the school plays. I began going by the name "Joe" instead of "Joey." I was trying so hard to not be my brother that I didn't know who I was trying to be.

I loved him, but I hated him. He was my best friend and my worst enemy. I admired and resented him. I wanted to be him. Yet I wanted nothing to do with him. With him around, there was no me. But without him, there was no us. And that was all I knew.

So when he came out to me one cool autumn night our senior-year of high school after a night of underage binge drinking, I wasn't ready. We sat there on the hill behind that little gym of our elementary school a block away from our house. He looked at me and I knew what was coming. This thing that had been eating away at me for so long was actually eating at him, too. But he was fine with it. And I wasn't. And I was left to deal with the fact that he was so comfortable in his shoes and mine felt like high heels three sizes too small.

I began coming out to family and friends as bisexual, partly because it felt easier than being gay, and partly because gay was another thing that became his. I tried to fill this void in myself through my unclear sexuality, without realizing that was only a small part of what was missing. Joe was just an act. But the more I played the part, the more I believed it was me.

We went to separate colleges, which allowed me to figure out my sexuality on my own. And that's when Joey started coming back. After college, my brother and I both moved to New York City. Our relationship flourished, and we were able to embrace our sexualities together, for the first time. But something still wasn't right. Even after letting go of a lifetime being attached to the strings of my parents and a formal education, I still felt like a marionette, just going through the motions. And I knew that I didn't want anyone else manipulating those strings anymore.

I didn't want to look in the mirror and see someone else. I wanted to see a story, a story that was mine. I wanted to be defined by my art (whatever that meant), by my love and by the tales that I had to tell that no one else did. I wanted to feel all that could be felt in this wide world beyond the walls of a closed closet door and the masks that others dressed me in.

I wanted to be able to sing a deep melody about battles lost and treasures found. I wanted to fall face first into a pile of my own mistakes and irresponsibly naïve decisions. I wanted to clear my own crooked path, not live in the shadow of someone else's.

It made sense to me why the reoccurring dreams that had haunted me since my childhood still lingered. And that's when I decided to run away from it all. I ran away from him. My parents. This idea of myself that I couldn't hold up any longer. I wanted to go to a place where no one knew my name (or my brother's). So I moved to New Orleans — trying to live the rebellious phase that I never had.

I bounced around from job to job, trying on different shoes. I became a waiter here, a bartender there, dealing with the internal judgment that my small hometown implanted in me for seemingly throwing away a college degree. But I knew I needed to start from scratch.

I began discovering this part of me that felt so strange yet oddly familiar. I started doing things people or society disapproved of, simply because it felt good. I intentionally stopped wearing deodorant one time after my manager indirectly commented on my "Bohemian" smell in front of the staff. My acting career was over.

And it was then that I started growing a beard. A long one. One that employers hated and my parents despised. It started out of laziness and grew organically into something much more than facial hair. It didn't really look good, but it made my adrenaline pump again. And that's when things started making sense.

I was empowered by others' reaction to the beard. It made some uncomfortable. Others judgmental. But there were those moments walking down the street or bussing tables where someone would stop and look at me — some black, some white, some men, some women. They saw that beard and all that it embodied, shooting me a compliment or a high five with a genuine smile. When they looked at me, I knew they saw me.

For the first time, I was able to see someone in the mirror that I've never really seen before. It wasn't my brother. Or that Joe guy. Or the good little boy in my childhood photos. It was this weird kid who had been waiting in that tiny gym all of his life to come out and play. And there he was. Staring back at me.

5. WE'RE DESPERATE

PATRICK GILL | SANTA CRUZ, CA

THE LAST TIME I put on Axe was to light myself on fire. I was making friends.

We sprayed half a can on each leg, Andrew probably used more. This was a month before I went straight edge for the next four years and two months into my first year of high school. Levi had already hit me in the face with a bottle of Olde English by accident, while he was pointing to something up in the tree line. It connected with my chin, sharp and round at the same time, but I couldn't really feel it. Connor got his lighter. We all took a gulp of malt liquor. The fire was like a spray of flowers, ones that bloomed early in the season, ones you didn't notice until you rode your bike again two hours later. There, in the clearing by Andrew's house, a momentary garden was blazing off our legs. We rolled on the dark wet grass. It might have been dew. It might have been the Olde English. We laughed, hoping the night wouldn't carry our laughter. It might wake up the neighbors. They were half a mile away, but still.

Three years before this I had moved from Scotts Valley to Aptos, nearly across the county but still deep in the same mountain range. I managed to stay at my same middle school through interdistrict haggling but would transfer for high school. Summers of Capitola Junior Lifeguards had built friendships with folks on this side of town, and a benefit of having older siblings is inherited acquaintances with their fellow siblings.

I was staying over at a new friend's place. Some say it's on the East Side, others say it's Midtown. If you look at a map, the East Side is West and the West Side is North; actual direction doesn't matter when you colloquially carve up hometowns. It depends on what you see and we all say. We were up Soquel Creek, veering off into the forest. We were deep enough for it to get dark quick but not so far that you couldn't walk to the liquor store. We were draining 40s bought by someone's brother. Four of us had the house to ourselves. We got drunk and lit ourselves on fire. What else do young men do?

Later we walked to the hill behind our high school. A few of us ran cross country. We had to scramble up that hill in the heat over and over again. At night we could take to the slope at our pace. We knew the trails by muscle memory — counting our steps and feeling the learned grooves underfoot. The tall grass arched further than our wide drunk stumbles.

By the top we were almost dry, done sloshing out philosophies — a lot of questioning of perception and existence. I am glad to have forgotten most of these conversations and too embarrassed to tell any I remember. It makes more sense under the influence of malt liquor and the stars. What else do young men do? Instead of talking, we nearly fell asleep at the top of the hill. Our sweat mingled with the dirt, and our backs were quietly gathering in dun and duff. We had to have been there for hours. That was the first night I realized the way alcohol distorts your perception of time.

Throughout high school, I hated the scent of Axe. Axe smells like desperation. It's a spray-on deodorant, essentially made for teenage boys who don't understand pheromones but want to smell like an accepted form of manhood. Axe's ads promise you access to feminine bodies — quiet until they chirp out their approval of your look, ravenous for your formidable cock. Axe could give you a lean body and a sneer, a playful sneer, a sneer that seduced and let you roll with whatever your average hyper-sexy-stud-but-still-approachable dude had to deal with. Like homework and bitches. You can see how much of a focus on bitches there was for young men — not quite fully realized women, bitches.

Axe is a pussy magnet in aerosol, carefully disheveled sex appeal for those who winced quietly or laughed when the cross section of female genitalia went up on the overhead in Health class. Even for boys who didn't think that hard about it, it was just what you wore at that age.

When I was in shape I was never toned, and for later admitted reasons, I could not relate to wanting women to lust after me. I was never an Axe man. I couldn't stand it. The thick and iridescent fog of it choked me when I went into the locker room for gym or weight training. Most varieties of it smelled simultaneously rich, dry, and sweet — like when your throat wells up with saliva before you vomit or like battery acid and posturing.

Odor aside, Axe stood for the masculinity I resented, the body and way of life I hated, while still desperately trying to prove my normativity. I wanted everyone to see my straightness — my value. But I didn't want to be the guy who sprayed a can of it on his weed-infused flannel before he got home late. I didn't want to be the guy who Xd himself with it throughout the day as if he thought it made his body a treasure map for the ladies.

I also didn't want to be the faggot. I didn't want to be set up with the only other out guy at the school. I didn't want to live with the expectations I saw him living with, beset with the mantel of Gossip Queen, Abercrombie clad, BFF for a tight triangle of girls who were pretty and nice enough — but not to be fucked with.

I needed something in what I saw as the middle that helped me maintain my burgeoning self-awareness. I tried using a deeper voice, stayed away from anything that could record it so that I would never have to feel the jagged pain of hearing how high it still was. I ratcheted my hips and made them as straightforward as possible while I walked. I tried to starve out or force out any fat that collected along those hips that might feminize me even more. I sweated out my sins on the track, on the soccer field and on the trails, punishing my body. I undernourished it, overfed it out of guilt to the point of bursting, ran it off and cut it off, all to sweat it off again. I held so tightly to the concept of letting it all go, an irony lost in my frantic lurching toward an ideal. I could do all that to myself, but I couldn't let one particle of spray deodorant touch me. Principles forged by youth are often misshapen.

*****

I have worked a series of hospitality jobs over the years. Hospitality is a fancy way of saying "service industry" — "food service" to be exact. I was the solitary baker covered in sweat, smoke, and flour; a crunchy vegan cook for an expensive juice bar; and a busser-cook-runner-dishwasher for a short while in a small but frightening café.

I have gravitated towards the front of the house, slowly. Though my hair is wild, my personal style reckless and my humor crass, I have an amiable face and disposition, one that's potentially comely. I show a dash of cool under pressure and am a small-talk genius. This is what a host should be. I clean up nice.

My years in the closet have taught me the importance of perception, but my work is still teaching me how and when to employ it. Yes, I can scrub up — but when, how and what polish is needed sometimes require direction. My current job is the first position I have had where I would be asked to leave for the day if I showed up in jeans. I wore jeans torn through the taint patched and re-patched ten times at some jobs, as long as I wasn't seen by guests.

I have been working at a Michigan Avenue restaurant: high volume, part-bar part-fine dining, great for private events or after work drinks, serving American Classics with global influences. Try the grilled cheese, with pork belly, a slice of heirloom tomato, and a fried egg. It's the perfect kind of decadent — best with a crisp lager. Imagine hearing all that in my "Hospitality Voice." It's the same one I use when I meet friends' parents. As a host, as your hear from interview onward, I am the first thing a guest sees. If I am not presentable, I am not doing my job. Strangely enough, I love it. Something about being up front, amongst the people, even if it's snippets of generic conversation with guests, is worth an often long and late shift on my feet.

A few weeks into my time there, I clocked in and was rifling through drawers behind our host counter. I think I was looking for pens; everyone steals pens. There was a canister of Axe in one drawer, right next to the perfume. I worked amongst a rank of tougher-than-they-look waifs with dark hair, amazons with mid-back length extensions and a simply chic short black outfit for every shift. In the dank air of eyebrow-raising sass, that makes the rich chuckle and slip you a tip, my wide-shouldered frame is masculine to their shades of femme. They are, to the tee, who they know they need to be. The Axe was for me.

That might seem rude to some people, like offering a mint to someone who is failing to cover up their halitosis. To me, it's a sign that my co-workers want me to step up. This says that they like me here and that I can stay if I am willing to work for my keep. This is the type of man you have to be — with slacks and shoes that compliment your belt but in a subtle way. You're a man who wears pressed shirts, hair combed into a style. The gesture is insurance against any hint of over-ripening — providing easy access can of spray-on deodorizing cologne. You are not the portrait of Axe; you are living as a man in an industry that doesn't accept "off" or less than polished.

There is a place and a time, where and when you compromise the smaller preferences or notions for a larger well-being. Outrage seems to come easier when you're young, at least it did for me. When rent and bills and groceries and clothing and your entertainment become something your pocket feels, you often grow a new perspective. By that time, you hope that you're bigger than that. Not everything requires a fight, you save a fight for a real attack on identity or on your community. You have developed a deeper sense of self.

Changing your appearance for a few short hours shouldn't cut the core like it used to. You can view it as choosing what you allow people to perceive of you — the surface. They see what you let them, but you ultimately are something beyond what they see. The outward appearance of your selfhood can manifest at your will. These are easily forgotten facts. It's the choice you've been making since high school, probably younger. I hope that with age I get better at it.

Every time I spray myself with Axe, I light myself on fire again. I redraw a character, from my skin and my heart. I am The Host, hospitality incarnate — but with some lovably rough edges. The heel of my thrift store shoes click, and I haven't had enough of a day off from any of my jobs to go down to the Marshall Fields building to get another pair with the gift card my Mom gave me for my birthday. I work hard, and I smile for you no matter what. I smile because I know I'm good at it.

It's me and it's not. It's an amplification yet still understated — cinched in at the waist while carrying two tubs of silverware on one hand and shoulder. It's strong because someone can scream in my face, dig their finger into my chest and I won't even blink. I will tell them that I am sorry for the miscommunication.

It wears Axe. I'm used to it.

6. LIKE THAT

NICO LANG | MILFORD, OHIO

I GREW UP IN a large high school in a small town, the kind of school that was known for good athletics and better academics. People from neighboring towns would cheat the system, saying that they lived in Milford to send their Honors Student to our school. In relative terms, Milford, Ohio was in the middle of nowhere. We knew we were considered "country folk," the name of our town said with an air of condescension by those who lived in Cincinnati proper — but at least we weren't Goshen or, God forbid, Owensville.

I'd never been to Owensville, but I knew that it was a place you didn't want to go, where the light doesn't touch. We were better. We were hicks, but we were hicks with a sense of class. I grew up in a trailer park, so I didn't know anything about that, only understanding wealth secondhand, living vicariously through photos of my friends' European vacations. They got cars when they turned sixteen. I got to ride on the bus again to school — just a little older this time. When I outgrew the other passengers around me, mostly freshmen and other underclassmen, I learned to walk along the highway to school or go through the woods.

The side of Milford I lived in was more diverse than the rest of our town — because we were poor — and I lived around working-class, immigrant and black families, the latter of which were a relative scarcity in our town.

It took me awhile to understand this, because I didn't realize what race was until a surprisingly late age. When I was growing up, my mother's best friend was black, and because we were always at each other's houses, I likewise became best friends with her daughter. I would play the Cowboy to her Indian, always ready to run after her and shoot her head off. Clearly I didn't get racism yet, and I didn't even realize it mattered that she and I were different.

I had no idea that difference was something you hated other people for until it was explained to me. I was at a wedding with my stepsister, accrued from my father's second marriage to a woman who lived down in Kentucky, where we spent our summers, and she asked me — out of the blue — if I would ever marry a black person. I thought of Lauren, my best friend, and all the fun we had together. Could I shoot her head off for the rest of our lives? I thought I was up to the task. "Sure!" I yelled. "Wouldn't you?"

Kicking up her pink flower girl dress, she laughed and made a choking sound of which I didn't understand the meaning. "No, that's disgusting," she said, twisting up her face as if her Shirley Temple had been replaced with horse semen. Ever the melodramatic child, I threw my hands up in the air and made a ripping gesture, tearing up the contract of our friendship. I told her we couldn't be friends anymore. "We're done," I barked.

My father quickly took me outside, grounding me for making a scene at the table. The issue here wasn't that we married into racism, but that I was making a big deal out of it. I didn't understand, because my parents allegedly taught me to stand up for what I believed in and what I thought was right.

Wasn't I right? My father told me it wasn't about that. I wondered what it was about.

Years later, my father divorced his second wife — of whom we now do not speak — and married a woman named Charice, a sort-of mail-order bride from the Philippines he met on the Internet. The thing is, though, I don't actually know if they are married. I assume so because a) they live together b) what's stopping them? and c) green cards are not that easy to get. I know this because I saw that Andie MacDowell movie with Gerard Depardieu. However, my father's never told me. I've asked him about it, many times, and he always says they aren't. I'm not so sure.

The first time I met her he told me she was the babysitter, and he's never bothered to ever tell my grandparents who she really is. When he came clean to me and told me they were together, he made me swear I would never tell them. "I think they figured it out by now," I said, but he vehemently shook his head. "Either way, just don't bring it up," he ordered. I asked him why. He told me that they wouldn't accept her. He sighed, "They're old, and they come from a different generation. Things were different back then."

This wasn't the first time I had heard this. I don't remember ever officially coming out to my father, but I assume that I had to, *right*? I remember him repeatedly asking me if I was "well, you know." He asked me in the car while we were listening to "Back Dat Ass Up," if memory serves, and he was pretending that he knew this song and that he was into it by moving his shoulders around and awkwardly gyrating like he was an eighth grader trying to twerk. He asked me again one morning while he was spreading potted meat on his sandwich.

Each time I said no. I didn't want to come out to him on his terms. I wanted to come out to him on mine, except that I don't remember when it happened. We don't remember 99% of our lives, but I wish I had kept that 1%. I wish I could visualize the look on my father's face when he knew that he knew, years of whispers and suspicions proved correct. I wish I could see his eyes to see what difference looked like.

However, I do remember our second conversation about it: "Don't tell your grandparents. They won't understand." We were sitting at the dining room table, one of many meals that were silent when they didn't have to be.

But I knew they knew, even if I didn't say it. I brought my boyfriend, Mark, around all the time. They set a plate for him at the dinner table and bought him presents on Santa's behalf every Christmas. He even got his own stocking one year, hanging right next to mine and almost touching. We've been broken up now for four years, but each year I find another gold-wrapped box with his name on it: "To Mark, From Santa." They told me they knew in a million ways, but they were just too polite to bring it up. Even if they didn't say it, they loved Mark because they loved me and loving him was a part of loving me.

But the thing that made Mark an acceptable houseguest was that he's white, unlike my father's possible secret wife. The year after Mark and I broke up, I brought another boy to Christmas, a skinny Kentuckian named Jesse with a gentle lisp and a silent disposition, as if he were too bashful to ever be the first to speak. Without really knowing him, my grandparents made sure there was a gift for Jesse underneath the tree.

In case he planned on sticking around, they wanted to make sure he didn't feel left out.

It's not the same with Charice, who occupies my grandparents' house like a ghost who lives in the attic. She and my grandmother never speak directly to each other. No one is under any illusion as to why. I listen to the way my grandmother talks about the black women with whom she and my grandfather work at the government job they've held for decades, forever connoted as being lazy and ignorant. It's the same tone they use to discuss their transgender co-worker, whose six-foot stature makes her an unmissable target for sideways gossip. Everything comes out in a whisper, as if they know they shouldn't be saying it too loudly. Someone might hear.

For my grandmother, there is something innate that divides us, a biological quality that makes black people inherently different, one unexplained by Achilles' heels or cocoa butter. I remember the white kids in my neighborhood who were so convinced that black people "smell funny," but I know for her, it's deeper than scent. I call my grandmother every day, and one day I told her that Walt Disney was a white supremacist, a fact I had recently learned and thought was worth mentioning. She told me that maybe he had a point.

My grandmother and I live in different Americas, ones that construct separate but overlapping histories; hers is an America where blacks continually abuse the system at the expense of whites, who are slowly being forced to give their power over to them, as if affirmative action were a plot in a spy movie. When I told her I saw *The Butler*, I mistakenly thought we might be able to discuss Oprah's performance in it. Everyone likes Oprah. However, she immediately derailed the conversation. She said, "I'm so sick of those movies being made."

I hoped she was talking about Oscar-bait movies, because I'm sick of those, too, but deep down, I knew what was about to happen. I asked her, "What kinds of movies, Nana?" and I waited. After considering her answer, she broke the silence, finally. She said, "No, movies about how bad *they* had it." Every time I want to close my eyes and forget we're different all over again, my grandmother reminds me.

However, I know that my grandmother doesn't know what she's talking about. She hasn't been lynched or had to drink at another fountain because people were worried her lips might contaminate her water. She's never had to go to a separate school or use the legal system to demand to go to the same school. She's never had an employer throw away her application simply because her name is "LaToya Davis" and the company doesn't want someone *like that* working at their company.

As an effeminate queer man who couldn't hide if I tried, I don't know what it's like to be a slave, but I do know what it's like to have people turn away from you because of who you are — the way you speak or the way you dress. When someone took a swing at me on the street for the simple fact of my identity, for swishing too much when I walk, I was reminded that I'm also *like that;* someone might not want me to exist, too. After all, my assailant didn't plan on missing his mark.

The thing is, though, that my grandmother also had to fight for her place in the world — both as a mother and a woman.

She grew up in a neighborhood poorer than mine, like something out of Frank McCourt, a place where she couldn't console herself by being higher on the social ladder than anyone. She had no one to feel better than. This was also the 1950s, a time when women could be legally raped by their husbands. She was abused by her second husband and cheated on by her third. She married her first husband, my grandfather, out of love — kind of — but it was just as much commerce as it was romance. My Nana was fourteen and looking for a way to provide for herself and her brothers and sisters, of which there were four. My grandfather was a Navy man, which meant steady income. It was food on the table.

My Nana's own father wasn't around and her mother couldn't handle taking care of the kids by herself. Her younger sister — my great aunt — required constant attention after their brother died in a car accident. She watched the life slowly drain out of the boy in front of her, as he bled out from the head. My aunt was seven years old, and the experience would scar her so badly that she never developed after that. She will be seven years old for the rest of her life. She will die the same little girl, just a much taller one.

The way people talk about my great-grandmother, I assume she lost her mind that day and never found it again. When I was a kid, both of my mother's other children were born with a genetic illness they never recovered from. My mother called them vegetables, but growing up, I didn't know what that meant. They didn't look like any cucumbers I had ever seen. Cucumbers didn't have faces and their eyes didn't close when they went to sleep. When my mother had to make the decision to pull the plug on each of them and remove the machines that kept them alive, I wondered what vegetable eyes look like when the lights go out inside. Do they stay open?

My family never recovered from those days, and our entire lives have been shaped by death. When you live in the shadow of loss, one of two things happen to you. You stay in the dark with the demons, like my mother has. You become dead along with them. Or you become my grandmother. You spend your entire life overcoming death, like a zombie who refuses to stay in the ground.

My Nana found a way not only to raise all of her brothers and sisters but also to raise her own children and to raise my brothers and me, all while holding down two to three jobs at a time. Whenever I ask her how she was ever able to do that, she tells me that she doesn't remember anymore. I think she just got so used to having to provide for everyone else around her that she didn't even think about it. Providing just became a trick of muscle memory. If you tap my grandmother's knee, she doesn't kick. She puts a gift under the tree.

I have nothing but love and overwhelming gratitude for this woman who raised me and who taught me what it was to be strong, and it pains me to think that someone who has been able to deal with so much in her life might not be able to see that other people are fighting, too. How could she be so blind to others' oppression? After everything she's been through, how could something as comparatively small as the race of her in-laws matter so much?

I know I could bring home as many men to Christmas as I wanted, but if I brought home a black man, that would be a very different story. I might as well kick the cat when I walked through the door. It's like the Jewish mothers who are okay with their kid being gay — so long as they don't date a Gentile. Sucking dick is fine. Eating heathen cock is another matter.

Other than Mark, my most significant relationship was with a Chicago Public School teacher — who I was on-again-off-again with for years, before he finally stopped letting me break his heart. Some bad relationships you can blame on your significant other and some are mutual. This was definitely my fault, but at the end of it, I was strangely relieved. Even if it did work out — and I could finally care for him the way I wanted to — I knew loving him wouldn't be so easy for my family.

This has long been a problem for me in my dating life, as I have a habit of attracting men of color. They think we're on the same team.

Being racially ambiguous, I'm often read as non-white or "vaguely ethnic," as a friend put it. Having a name like "Nico Lang" certainly doesn't clear up the confusion. I've been mistaken for Chinese, Japanese, Filipino, Latino, Jewish, Middle Eastern, Greek and just about everything you can think of. A man once grabbed my butt at a conference and said, "Oh, baby. You must be Puerto Rican." I responded, "I'm not anything." He laughed. "You're always something to somebody, even if you don't know it."

I have a friend who is half-black and doesn't look it at all, her Greek heritage overpowering any visual manifestation of her ethnicity. She gets White Privilege, even though she isn't actually white, a living testament to race as both reality and perception. I'm perceived to be something, and people can't figure out what that something is. When I come out to guys as "nothing" and pull out my White Privilege card, they always seem vaguely disappointed. I'm just another white activist and social justice fetishist who thinks he knows about race. "I'm learning," I always respond.

Like most people, my grandmother hasn't been taught to think critically about race, and I wonder sometimes if my grandmother thinks of herself as being racist. I highly doubt it. When you get to my Nana's age, experiencing everything she has, you feel like you've earned your opinions. You've lived enough life to be entitled to what you think and not have to apologize for it. No one her age looks in the mirror and says, "I'm a racist. I am bigoted. I have prejudiced views that are harmful to others." No one says that at any age.

Yet each of us who are born white and operate within a system of power and privilege are racist, in subtle ways that we don't notice. We're like fish that swim in racist water, not able to see the bubbles of prejudice in what we breathe. It surrounds you and gets inside you.

In that system, racism isn't just twisting your mustache and cackling or spitting in someone's face. It's complacency and ignorance, a process of fighting your way to the surface as best you can. I've made a million excuses for myself when I don't make it all the way there, but how often do I give my Nana the opportunity to learn to swim? I'm beginning to think my father and I doing a disservice to her by keeping her away from the issue, if we still aren't trusting her to keep fighting the current she was born into.

When I eventually came out to my grandmother, she said she wanted to say something to me. She was just waiting until I was ready. She knew since I was four. I asked what tipped her off, and then I remembered putting on a live performance of a Britney Spears routine in my 8th grade English class, complete with full song and dance. I spent weeks at home memorizing the choreography, and my grandmother helped me practice. She even bought me the CD, smiling as I played the same song over and over again.

I remember how badly I wanted to go to Britney concert and how my grandmother offered to take me — just the two of us. But after being teased for listening to my Britney CD on the bus, I didn't want to go, because "it wasn't what boys did." My grandmother told me, "You can be any kind of boy you want."

Some kids have to come out. I was never in.

Harvey Milk used to say that the reason queer people need to come out is so that we can stand up and be counted for who we are. Being our authentic selves in public, as flamboyant or brilliant as the fire with we were made, allows people to get to know us. Queer people are much harder to discriminate against when they aren't just the people on television but your neighbors, your friends and your relatives.

Since coming out, I've given my grandmother the opportunity to know the real me, but every moment I stay in the dark about race, I'm not being authentic. I'm still the kid who got grounded for speaking up. I'm still the one who is too afraid of punishment to make things a little uncomfortable. Over time, I learned to be quiet.

When I look at my grandmother, I know that racists aren't just the people we see on TV, ones standing at picket lines to block the way of progress. Racism is also nice people who are so busy trying to be nice that we don't have a real conversation, scared that we might raise the dead. Racism is a deeper and more complicated issue than anything we've been taught, one that doesn't go away when we pretend it doesn't exist.

My Nana might have a race problem, but so do I.

7. INSIDE MAN

R.J. AGUIAR | TALLAHASSEE, FLORIDA

AS I PLACED THE Tupperware container in the microwave, I could already hear my co-workers in the next room chatting and snickering away. I start pressing away at buttons and let out a labored sigh. I had already made sure to start my lunch late, trying to time it perfectly so that they were wrapping up as soon as I was just starting mine. I could quickly and pleasantly put in my brief face-time without feeling obligated to take part in whatever mindless gossip they were discussing that day. Judging from the sound of their excited chatter, though, it didn't sound like they would not be wrapping up any time soon. My eyelids closed, concealing the gigantic eye roll taking place underneath. On the one hand, I'm starving and anxious to eat my food. On the other, I know that the second that microwave beeps they'll be expecting me.

I carry my Tupperware container into our combination file/conference/break room just as the group is caught in one of their fits of laughter. One co-worker, an inane recent divorcee we'll call "Denise," is the first to spot me. "Hi, R.J.!" she calls out just a little too enthusiastically, strained smile beaming across her face. This prompts muffled greetings from the rest of the group in between bites of Lean Cuisine and cafeteria meatloaf. My eyebrows perk up as I force a placid smile on my face. "Hey guys," I say softly, as I find an open seat at the massive wooden table. The group's ringleader, a large and boisterous small-town woman we'll call "Mary," asks me, with a playfully aggressive tone, "So whatcha got today?" I sheepishly reply, "Spaghetti squash with chicken and paleo pesto." The group rolls their eyes and chuckles, shooting glances to each other that say "Who does this guy think he is?"

Another colleague, a rotund but demure Southerner named "Vicki," slides a sheet of paper over to me. It's just then that I notice that the entire group has been passing around sheets of paper. Sometimes, when members of the group find humorous jokes and anecdotes online, they'll print them out for all of the others to read. These are, no doubt, what the group has been laughing about. I pick it up, thankful for the opportunity to sit in silence and not make conversation.

I pour through various bland, watered-down anecdotes and jokes, half of which I've already seen in various chain emails throughout the early 2000s. "Yesterday is history, tomorrow is a mystery, today is a gift. That's why it's called the present!" The paper mistakenly attributes the quote to Ronald Reagan, and I chuckle quietly to myself for all the wrong reasons. "If you're not liberal by the time you're 18, you don't have a heart. If you're not conservative by the time you're 30, you don't have a brain." I know that the quote isn't by Winston Churchill, which is what the paper says, but I decide not to say anything.

I take a look at the next paper, which contains those little pseudo-philosophical observations that still puzzle us as adults. "Why does the sun make your skin darker and your hair lighter?" "Why is it that, in order to get a loan, you have to first prove that you don't need one?" "If we supposedly evolved from monkeys, then why are there still monkeys?"

"I know the answer to this one," I announce before I can stop myself.

Shit.

Everyone stops and looks over at me. "Which one?" asks Mary. I know I shouldn't answer, but I've already opened my mouth. I search the rest of the page, looking for another question that I can make work. "How does Jell-O go from solid to liquid to solid again?" I remember Googling the answer one day, but can't remember it well enough to explain it now. "If time heals all wounds, why does it eventually kill us all?" People spend their whole lives answering that. Finally I break down. "This one, the monkey one." I point to it on the paper and slide it over in Mary's direction. It takes her a second, but I know the instant that she realizes which one I'm talking about. "Well yeah, because we didn't," she laughs, as if she just solved 2 + 2. I look around at the rest of the group, all sending looks my way that say "Yeah, of course" and "Didn't you know that?" I take a deep breath. Do I really want to start this conversation? I can't see it ending particularly well. They already expect an answer from me. Besides, maybe if I can articulate my position a certain way, it'll help change their perspective a little bit. It's a longshot, but I'm already committed.

"Well, you're right in that we didn't evolve from the same monkeys that exist today. We came from a common ancestor. So it's not like we came from chimpanzees or anything. We're just related to them because we share a common origin."

"So why did we start evolving to be different?" challenges Mary, almost before I can finish. I can tell that she expects me to concede after this one counter-argument. I know that I made a mistake already, but now I'm to the point where I'm continuing the argument to save face. "Why do any two species evolve differently? Most of the time, it's because two large groups get separated and then adapt over time to their new separate environments." My answer prompts a quiet hiccup of laughter from Vicki. Mary jumps in again: "So then where's the missing link?"

"What do you mean?" I ask back. Mary looks emboldened, convinced that she's cornered me. "The missing link. Where's the missing link that connects us to monkeys?" I can't help but fire back a look that says: "Are you serious?" "They've found evidence of like four or five already. Have you heard of Lucy?

The one that they found some years ago." The room is silent. There's a mixture of expressions staring back at me. A couple seem amused by my response. Others look convinced that I'm trying to stir up trouble. "Haven't you guys seen any of the diagrams where they compare the different skull shapes?" Silence. I know I'm fighting a losing battle now. No one in the room seems to be at all receptive to anything that I have to say.

There's a long and excruciating pause. I retreat to my leftovers, powerless against the wall of willful ignorance in front of me. I hear shuffling as Vicki gathers the papers that are scattered about the table. Meanwhile, everyone else is gathering up their things and leaving. The conversation isn't finished, though, until Mary adds a coy "Oh well, agree to disagree" before leaving the room. I get out my phone and hop on Twitter, trying to dull the frustration that's currently boiling in my brain.

*****

When you look at Florida's state government from the outside, it's a pretty grotesque sight. I come from a state with a governor who was elected after running the most expensive gubernatorial campaign in the state's history. His campaign, which preached fiscal responsibility, was largely financed by funds from a healthcare company that forced him to resign after it was being investigated by the Internal Revenue Service and the Department of Health and Human Services. The governor's biggest accomplishments thus far include rejecting federal funding for high speed rail and forcing welfare applicants to submit drug tests (a program that proved both illegal and ended up costing the state money). The state's Attorney General is a former Fox

News analyst whose most noteworthy accomplishment is unsuccessfully suing the federal government and repealing the "Obamacare" law. They also oppose same-sex marriage, for what it's worth.

Imagine my apprehension, then, when I first found out that I would be working for the Florida's Office of the Attorney General. As a gay Latino who came from immigrant parents and a pretty modest background, it seemed like one of the worst places on Earth for me to work. Believe me, I wouldn't have taken that job if there were any better options available. Unfortunately, when you graduate college in the worst economy since the Great Depression, you're not exactly swimming in job offers...especially when you double major in Media Production and Creative Writing. Still when confronted with the choice between working for Republicans and being a barista at Starbucks, I definitely had to give it some thought. At least the gig at Starbucks could've landed me with some kind of health care or benefits.

But suffice it to say, spending two years making lattes after graduating Magna Cum Laude does not look good on a resume. As much as it would pain me to serve the very politicians who seemed hell bent on screwing me over as often as possible, at least I wouldn't have future employers turning up their nose at my prior work experience.

I'd love to say that my two years inside gave me an intimate knowledge of the sinister inner workings of the state's Attorney General or the Governor's master plans. I wish I could say that I now know what sort of sinister and incompetent schemes they're about to set in motion. The truth is actually far less swashbuckling and far more depressing than I originally thought, but that doesn't necessarily make it any less troubling.

See, the Attorney General doesn't even work in the building that's dubbed the "Attorney General's Office." Her office is safely removed, two blocks away at the State Capitol building, where she and only a very select group of staffers get to do their work tucked away from everyone else. To say that the staff is removed would be a bit of an understatement, since we peons weren't even allowed to send them emails without approval from two bosses up. One could easily spend years working for the Attorney General's office without ever actually meeting the general face to face, or even physically laying eyes on them.

During my two years there, I interacted with the Attorney General about six times, only four of which were in person and two of which were in the actual office. Just about every time I did see her, she was always flanked by at least two members of her staff. While I know that bringing an entourage is common among politicians, hers seemed to be poised at all times to step in, just in case she started saying something a little too dense or airheaded.

The Attorney General's removal from her staff didn't stop a few pieces of information from trickling over. I know that she brings her St. Bernard, Luke, with her to work just about every day — to a building that doesn't allow any animals except service animals. Word has it that she was also using her interns to walk and clean up after Luke until she was finally told to hire her own handler. I've also heard independently from multiple co-workers that the woman is a bit of a pill popper, despite being a champion to end prescription drug abuse.

These are idle bits of gossip, though, and they are certainly not what I found to be the most troubling during my time as a state employee. However sinister or blatantly incompetent people like them may seem, they all come and go. Meanwhile, all of the low and mid-level drones stay behind, often for decades upon decades at a time. The thing with conservative governments is that they care more that it's being run cheaply than they do about it being run well. State government doesn't aggressively recruit the best and brightest — they don't have the money. Any young and talented person I encountered at the Attorney General's office was in my situation. They were facing bleak career prospects, simply biding their time until they could move on to something better. This reality was made worse by the fact that the state abuses a classification called OPS (or Other Personal Services). On paper, OPS employees are supposed to be like independent contractors, and are only supposed to be used for jobs that are temporary and related to a specific task that needs to be completed. That's how the state can justify not giving them any sort of benefits whatsoever and keeping them as completely at-will employees who can be fired without reason at any time. As an OPS employee, I worked the same full time hours as my non-OPS counterparts and was expected to put in the same effort without enjoying any of their benefits like health care, sick leave, or any sort of paid time off. The guy who had my job before me was there for four years before he left, and my same position still exists even after I left two years later.

Of course, no one cares about the blatant misuse of OPS employees except OPS employees. Any complaints typically fall on deaf ears. A vast majority of other employees are too indifferent or complacent to care. "No one forced you to take this job," they'll typically reply. "If things are really so bad here, then just go and find a job somewhere else." These responses are, of course, coming from employees who have occupied their same seat for years at a time. If you're not the few elite employees at the very top, the only way for you to obtain a stable pay rate with benefits and such is to stay put for as long as you can. Look around state employees' offices, and you'll notice that merit awards are in extremely short supply. Instead you'll see various plaques and nick-nacks that read "5

Years" or "10 Years" or "20 Years" or "25 Years." The system rewards loyalty and mediocrity rather than achievement, creating a culture that embraces one mindset: "Sit down, shut up, do what you're told, and don't make any trouble." Plop someone like me — someone who is gay, Hispanic, liberal, opinionated, and outspoken — in that system, and it becomes very clear that being different can be dangerous. Having lived it for two years, I can say that it's been one of the most frustrating, draining, and alienating experiences of my life.

First off, Florida is one of the 34 states where it is perfectly legal to fire someone for being gay. While the Attorney General's Office does have a policy that prohibits discrimination based on sexual orientation and gender identity, there's no real law that would protect you should they choose not to obey that policy. Not to mention the fact that the policy doesn't really matter when you can already be fired at any time for no reason whatsoever. That is not to say that I was at all closeted during my time as a state employee. As a matter of fact, most of my co-workers knew my boyfriend personally and were perfectly cordial when it came to our relationship.

That said, I would certainly get some sideways glances any time someone saw me reading *The Advocate*'s webpage, which was one of the very few LGBT news sites that wasn't blocked by our system. At one point, I even had to explain that *The Advocate* was a news publication and not the kind of "inappropriate website" that some of my co-workers were whispering behind my back. A vast majority of my supervisors and colleagues didn't care at all about my gay relationship.

That said, when our local news wanted to interview me and my boyfriend on the day of the DOMA and Prop 8 rulings, I was told explicitly to keep my status as a state employee completely under wraps.

I'm not saying that I was singled out by my colleagues for being gay, or for being Latino or Liberal or anything like that. All of these characteristics were simply reasons why I was "different," and when you're a state employee who has been used to business as usual for the past one or more decades, people who are "different" can also come across as threatening. This is how we arrive at scenes like the one that I previously described.

Sure, it's easy to find such differences in opinion amusing, but when your opinions and education only serve to single you out even more, you can see just how potentially precarious they can be. This is especially true when certain co-workers are already sowing seeds of discord behind your back. Over and over, I found myself called into my supervisor's office so that she could tell me to "tone down" my demeanor — because it was somehow proving problematic for my co-workers. However, insulting talks like that may prove to be, they can be especially stressful when you're the one wearing the red shirt on the Starship Enterprise. They're even worse when you're underpaid salary and lack of healthcare and benefits leaves you with virtually no financial safety net should your superiors finally decide that you're too much trouble and decide to get rid of you.

Every morning, when I traversed the bleak, taupe hallways, climbed the bleached-white stairwell, and navigated the cluster of drab, gray cubicles to finally arrive at my own desk, I could always feel my pulse quickening.

Government buildings, or at least the one I worked in, typically aren't the teeming beehives you see portrayed on movies and TV. Mine was quite the opposite. It was a filing cabinet packed to the brim with low and mid-level slaves just counting down the hours until they could finally be set free. I used a polite veneer to gloss over my feelings of frustration and anxiety. Those emotions will continue to plague you until you finally allow them to "break" you, and convince you that it's easier and clearly better to resign yourself to the imperfect system rather than do anything to change it.

Dealing with that kind of oppression day in and day out gets to you. I would find myself returning home from work and already snapping at my boyfriend within the first few minutes of my arrival. For several months, I found myself in a depressive state and in a creative roadblock, unable to do any of the writing at home that had previously brought me so much joy and catharsis. My health started to deteriorate, worsening my anxiety — since every sick day I took would already eat away at my financial well-being. Every meeting or "coaching session" with my supervisor put my heartbeat in my throat and would sometimes even cause fits of nausea and vomiting. God forbid my fits of nausea would keep me away from my desk for too long, though, lest my co-workers start to ask questions about my extended bathroom breaks.

Over and over, my boyfriend and my other friends would ask me why I took everything at work so personally. I couldn't help it, though, since I'm the kind of person who throws himself into everything that he does.

I wasn't the only gay person working for the Attorney General's office — not by a long shot. However, there were plenty of gay people there who weren't nearly as open about their relationships or personal lives as I was. I knew of at least two fellow gays who didn't feel comfortable revealing their orientations to their bosses. The AG's office does have a policy in place that prohibits discrimination based on sexual orientation, but it can only do so much. These co-workers of mine still felt like it was easier to stay closeted than risk being singled out as "different," especially those who could already be fired at any time, with or without reason.

My situation, unfortunately, was not particularly uncommon. Time after time, I watched plenty of young and talented people, many far more intelligent and talented than I, jump ship. Almost none of them were even gay; they had just managed to be singled out by their co-workers for other reasons. Many had bosses who mistook their competence for arrogance or saw their new ideas as a threat to the status quo. This environment is designed to make you expendable, so the people who are able to find better opportunities elsewhere leave as soon as they get the chance. Some, like myself, are even willing to take a substantial decrease in income just to get out. All that remains are the people who aren't qualified to find better work elsewhere and have to face the reality of either conforming or continuing to put them at risk.

The thing is, I don't really fault a lot of my former co-workers for perpetuating a mindset that's hostile to change. After all, they've been indoctrinated into this mindset throughout the entirety of their careers. It's a kind of pack mentality that can overwhelm any person's most benevolent tendencies. They are right, after all — it is easier to go with the flow. It is easier to go along with a flawed system than it is to try and fix it. A vast majority of them meant no ill will be anything that they said and did. A vast majority of them are truly good people.

It's extremely easy to examine the hijinks of people like Governor or the state's Attorney General or other politicians and condemn their actions and the actions of those working beneath them. But know that, in reality, there are hundreds and sometimes thousands of people working underneath them and that they may simply be steering ships that have already been sinking for years. Fixing a system like the one in Florida requires more than simply electing the right leaders, which is already a tall order for your average American voter. Many times, there's no way to tell that a ship is sinking until you've ridden on it and seen the water level creep up, and even then, the water may be creeping up too slowly for you to notice. It's even worse when you're on a ship that's sinking, but warning other passengers can very well get you thrown overboard.

I knew that, when I first took that job, that I would become part of a broken system for a brief period of time. I had absolutely no how endemically flawed that system would be. Worse yet, most of the people who know that fact have already abandoned ship.

8. TESTOSTERONE FUELED INJECTION

BUCK ANGEL | YUCATAN, MEXICO

I ALWAYS WANTED TO be a man. I wanted to smell like a man. Taste like a man. Fuck like a man. This might seem like a really weird thing to say coming from a man, but I was not always a man. I've always felt like one, just born in a body that said something different than what I wanted it to.

Many years ago I had the opportunity to change my gender. Back in the day, we called it a "sex change," but today it's called "transformation" or "transitioning." After many years of self-hatred and abuse to my body, including suicide attempts, I started taking testosterone in my late 20s. When I finally realized that I could change my gender through the use of testosterone, I was all over it.

I remember the first injection from my doctor vividly. I was his very first transsexual male patient — which put me into a whole new world. I know that I was imagining more than was actually physically happening after that first shot, but that didn't matter to me. All that mattered was that I knew my life as a man was about to start.

Month after month I started to notice little changes. My voice began to sound like a 16-year-old boy; it was squeaky, like going through puberty again. I started growing hair in places that I had never had before. Even my face started to change with my jaw line and nose. Most of all, I started losing my hair on my head. At first, that was hard, but once I just realized how masculine that made me look, I went with it and just shaved it off.

Along with muscles, facial hair was (and still is) one of the things I always longed for. The testosterone gave me that. I worked very hard on my body at the gym and started developing a new male figure. Where there once were skinny arms and legs now grew new muscles. I was shaped like a man. Surgery came about two years into the testosterone. I opted to get my chest surgery first, choosing a brand new surgery that worked very well for me and left no scars. It enabled me to build my chest at the gym so that it totally developed into a male chest.

At the time, the hardest decision for me was not getting "bottom surgery," the operation that transforms your biological vagina into a semi-functional penis. Deciding that the "cock" was not for me, I chose to stay with what I was born with. I became a man with a pussy. It was a hard and sensitive thing for me to get my head around, but with time I became proud of my self-made body.

Besides, the hormones were enough of an adjustment.

You see, taking testosterone into a body that physically didn't produce it made me feel sexually charged in a way I'd never felt before, like being a teenage boy for the first time. All I could think about was sex with women — but then suddenly guys were on my mind, too. The testosterone was so powerful that it began directing my sexual fantasies toward men. It was shocking at first, but as I became more comfortable in my body, I knew I could not fight this urge for cock.

With this, I entered the world of gay male sex.

One day, I finally got the nerve to go to a leather bar in my town to explore my sexuality more. When I arrived at the local leather bar, I immediately felt like a whole new world opened up. *Wow*, I thought, *I am home.* Looking back I think this was one of those moments that helped define myself as a man: the raw masculine energy in the leather bar, having sex without a care in the world. I had never experienced such a thing in my life.

But that was just the beginning.

*****

I walked in and noticed that all the guys were watching me with that hungry look. I felt totally out of my comfort zone — scared yet at the same time so horny for what I was hoping would happen. I had experience with the leather scene — but not as a man, only as a butch girl.

I made my way up to the bar and ordered a club soda. I stopped drinking years ago, but I was so nervous that I wished I could order just one. Lots of guys were just standing around — some kissing each other and some staring at me or the other guys in the bar. I noticed guys rubbing each other's cocks through their jeans or tight leather pants, but what I really picked up on were the guys going to and from a room near the back. Of course, I knew what was going on in there and really wanted to head over but couldn't get myself to move in that direction.

Suddenly, I heard a guy behind me say, "Hey buddy, haven't seen you in here before." I turned to see a dude with the most amazing mustache smiling at me. I thought, "Now what do I do?" I said back, "Hey, buddy." That was all I needed to do. As soon as we started talking, I could feel the sex.

We talked about the little things like where we're both from, what you say to waste time before you get to the real talk. Eventually he asked me: "What are you into?"

"Cigars, piss and boots," I responded — because that really was the first thing that came to my mind. Before I knew it, we were outside on the patio starting to smoke a big fatty. I couldn't believe this was happening — this hot dude in tight Levis with knee high boots and no shirt, smoking a cigar with me. So then he asked me if he could "worship my boots." "Really?" I asked, already knowing my answer. "Of course, you fucking can."

He got on his knees and started licking my leather with such a passion that my pussy began to ache with sex. My little cock began to pulse and grow as he licked away. I saw the desire in his eyes. I saw his cock, which was bulging out of his tight jeans. I started getting more and more turned on — when all of a sudden I realized that this might go farther than just a boot-licking session. I had a choice I needed to make here. Should I tell him that I am a man with a pussy? Or should I just let it go and see what happens?

I am the type of guy who's all about truth and honesty. I didn't feel like it would be cool if I didn't say anything, and it could have possibly turned into a bad situation if we got down and dirty and my pussy was a problem for him, which I was almost sure it could be.

So with all my might, I reached down and grabbed him by the hair, whispering in his ear. "Just to let you know: I have a pussy," I told him. "I am a transsexual man." He moved back from me and looked up, still on his knees and said, "I don't understand." Of course he didn't. Trying not to ruin it, I said, "I was born female but had a sex change to a man and kept my pussy. If you're still interested in playing that would be cool, but if not, I totally understand and we can just move on. No hard feelings, buddy."

He looked at me and replied, "Well, this is totally new to me but you're super hot and you feel like a man to me. I would love to still play — if that's okay with you, sir."

It was on. No looking back now. My first sex experience in a men's only place was happening — now.

I pushed his head back down to my boots, where he began to lick. My crotch continued to grow and get wet. My boot wandered to his hard cock and started to rub it as he looked up at me with puppy-dog eyes. I forced his head into my hard pussy and he started sniffing and licking through my jeans. With the cigar in my mouth and this boy in my crotch, I felt like the manliest man on earth. I told him to come up to me. We started to kiss with such force that his mustache was burning my face. It felt so good.

The taste of cigars and sex was all over us. I started to rub his hairy chest with my hands looking for his nipples as he asked permission to do the same on me. We rubbed on each other like this for so long that I lost track of time. Eventually I looked up and saw guys watching us. This made me feel weird, as I was so not used to public sex. However, I shut my eyes and continued to play with this boy. The feeling of man-on-man sex was something I had been longing for during all my jack-off fantasies. Now it was really happening.

I so wanted to feel his cock in my mouth and his mouth on my pussy with that big thick mustache rubbing on my belly.

I could feel the heat coming off our bodies, as we continued to kiss and rub all over each other. I grabbed him by the neck and looked him in his eyes. "Open your mouth," I commanded, flicking my cigar ash into his dark hole. He thanked me. I told him that we were going to another room. "Are you okay with that?" I asked. Even though I was still nervous, it was as if I knew what I was doing all along. I guided him by the neck to the back room where it was dark but light enough that I could see lots of other guys sucking each other off. The air was filled with their sounds.

I had no fucking idea what I was going to do. I just knew that I should go to this room and see what happens.

So I put him on his knees again and told him to start licking my boots. I unbuttoned my Levis slowly, so scared and so hard at the same time. My pussy was wet with excitement. I pushed him down just enough to let him meet my hard pussy before pushing his head toward it. I do this not too forcefully just because I am still convinced he's going to freak out on me. However, he slowly moves towards me and starts to suck my hard little cock. "Oh, shit!" I yelped. "Shit." I've never felt anything like this before. His moustache rubbed me, and his mouth sucked me so hard; with all this friction, he was about to make me cum all over his face.

I pushed him back and asked him if he was enjoying himself. He responded, "Please sir, may I continue?" I pushed him back in.

As I was experiencing this amazing feeling I opened my eyes and saw a couple guys come over to watch us. This just made it hotter for me. My nervousness turned into aggressiveness, and I started fucking his face while the other guys started to kiss me and play with my nipples. I wasn't sure if they realized that he was sucking on my pussy or not, but no one seemed to give a shit. I didn't give a shit. And then in that moment, I came.

I pushed him off of my pussy and pulled my Levis up. The other guys had their bulging, hard cocks in their hands stroking, all so fucking hot. I pushed my boy towards them and he started to suck one guy while I kissed and played with their nipples. I wanted to suck cock so bad, but I didn't feel confident enough to go there just yet. So I didn't.

I continued to play as the boy sucked them, and slowly I removed myself from the group and re-entered the front of the bar — in some kind of sex haze. I felt like I needed to leave before I was found out. I am not sure why, but I suddenly felt uncomfortable, leaving in a rush, never to see that guy again.

I still think of him. I wonder if he thinks of me.

9. FOR COLORED BOYS WHO LOVE WHITE BOYS

MADISON MOORE | NEW YORK/PARIS

1

A FEW YEARS AGO I was on a gay dating site and this guy wrote me a friendly message. It all happened so long ago that I forgot what common come-on line he used exactly, but I do remember that in the course of our conversation he asked if I wanted to have sex — right now. This was not an unusual request in these parts. I told him "No," and his response has stuck with me for years.

"Ugh, you are so sad," he told me. "Another black guy who is racist against his own people!" He blocked me immediately. I didn't even get the chance to reply.

I couldn't believe it. Clearly this guy was going through something, having been burned any number of times by guys, black and otherwise, who are not into black guys. But that's not why I wasn't interested in him. He just wasn't my type. I don't know, he just seemed dull. I could barely finish his profile because I actually fell asleep reading it. But his message still bothers me today, mostly because it makes a gay male truth painfully clear: that the majority of gay men in America have a race problem.

In some ways, however, my Angry Blocker was right. I've never dated a black guy. Sean, Max, Trevor, Tyler* – a grand total of eleven years of relationships with white boys. That's a ton of pink cock. Since most people date within their own race anyway, often for familial or other cultural reasons, the lack of diversity in my dating pool probably doesn't come as too much of a shock. But I'm a black gay man who has never dated a black guy, and it's a topic I'm pretty sensitive about.

I love white boys, but it's not like if you're white that's all you need to get with me. To be clear I love all boys: like, if you are a total top and have a huge/nice penis, call me.

When I was with Max, he would do something and I would go, "You are so white!" and it was a funny thing we teased each other about. When I see a white guy I'm attracted to, I instantly notice his hands and how they are different from mine. I love the way our hands look when we lock them together and I love staring into eye colors that are foreign to me. I love that they are so unlike mine. It's the disparity that turns me on.

Over the years I've seen my "type" of guy become increasingly specific. You need to be skinny, and I hate muscles and guys with too much muscle. I don't give a shit if you're "straight acting" or if a purse falls out of your mouth when you speak — because I'm probably the only gay guy on the earth who thinks a femme top is kind of hot. I'm also attracted to tall skinny guys who wear tight jeans, maybe they're tatted, maybe they have long hair or a half-shaved head or plays in some dumb band or otherwise works in the creative field. Basically I'm only attracted to hipsters and artsy, creative types.

My best friend (a black gay) and I were talking the other day about how conflicted I am about liking white guys, as if there's something wrong with me and I'm not supposed to be this way. He told me if I'm attracted to hipsters, not just white guys; the brown hipsters are harder to find, but they are there if you're looking. And he's right. I sent him an emergency text message a few days ago because I saw this *so hot* Latino guy on the subway, tall (check), skinny (check), arms covered in tattoos (check), septum piercing (check) and he was carrying a skateboard (bonus!).

I spent my late elementary and early middle school years with my grandmother in Saint Louis, Missouri. Everyone thought the cool kids in my grade were the popular kids who fit in and who everybody liked. However, I was always drawn to a much darker scene. I was interested in the less popular punk rock kids — the scene kids who wore black, played music and dotted their eyes in eyeliner, were the first to get tattoos, had strange haircuts and probably pierced their own ears. There was something really interesting to me about them, something edgy and urgent. Everybody else tried to fit in, and I was drawn to them because they didn't fit in. Though I wasn't really a part of their group, I watched from afar and sort of wished I could be like them.

That's the thing about desire: we fashion ourselves after what we're attracted to, even when we don't know we're doing it. It's like a reciprocal dance. Some guys go to the gym to bulk up because they want a muscle top/bottom. In the last few years I've gotten tattoos and gauged my ears because I find that look sexy on other people, but also because I know it means something to people who like that look, too. That's why you often see two guys dating with totally similar styles. They're sending out a message about themselves with what they're wearing. They're saying, "Hey, I'm safe. You can date me because I'm just like you."

But sometimes becoming "like" someone just to get them to notice you can be really stressful. When I was a teenager I used to get so mad when I saw boys of color trying to dress like white boys to attract white boys. You would go to the mall, or even gay spaces, and see so many twinky bleached haired brown boys wearing Abercrombie shirts, as if trying to say, "Hey, I'm safe. You can date me because I am just like you – even though I'm brown." Abercrombie was such a thing when I was a gay teenager that people would use the term "AFBoi" in their screen name to describe themselves. "Abercrombie" and "AF" was code for white. I think it still is.

The problem is that brown boys often love white boys, but white boys don't always love brown boys — especially not in America. I don't think white guys think about or realize how much it affects people when they specify which races they aren't into. However, they don't have to think about that, because they are already the center of power around which the entire mainstream gay world circulates. Brown boys all over know what its like to feel invisible in this marketplace of desire. You start to feel ugly because you write some hot white guy and his profile says, "NO BLACKS." You get skeptical of anyone who is interested in you because you think they only want you for the huge cock they imagine you have, or they automatically assume you're a top just because you're black. You identify yourself as black on Grindr but some guy sees you and takes it upon himself to tell you that "you aren't fully black, you're mixed with something" as if, somehow, that makes you better.

A few days ago I saw a screenshot of some guy's Grindr profile on a blog and it said: "Not interested in black guys." The thing is that this guy was black. I couldn't believe it. How could somebody express such specific disinterest in their own race like that? Though, to be fair, I do know plenty of white gay guys who specifically do not date white gay men. However, what made it even worse is that somebody in the comments said, "I wouldn't fuck a black guy either. He's just being honest. If you are attractive enough to *get* a white guy, why settle?"

If you are attractive enough to "get" a white guy? Is the market value of white gay men that valuable? Even though I've never dated a brown guy before, I have also never, ever said "No black guys" or listed shelves of races I wasn't into. I just don't use race to close myself off to people that way.

2

Race is such a problem in the gay world that I didn't even know people thought I was attractive until I moved to Paris for a few years when I was in college. That's how lonely and isolated I felt in the American gay world. Not because I felt that I was actually ugly but more that I sensed that my being black would always be a minus.

When I first set foot in Paris almost a decade ago now, I learned that boys of every race thought I was attractive – including North African guys, who are hot as shit. I could barely move down the street without some new person trying to get it in, and I'm putting it this way because it was actually as aggressive as I'm making it sound. I was asked to model. I was asked to be in porn. There was the hot guy at my Arabe du coin, a bodega in my neighborhood, who asked me to suck him off every time I went in the store. There was the taxi driver who told me I wouldn't have to pay my fare if I gave him head. Man, French guys really like blowjobs. Then there was the guy who squeezed my ass cheeks to eternity on a crowded subway car. There was no shortage of guys interested in me anywhere in France or Europe more broadly. It was all very exciting because at 20 years old, in my, let's say, five years of being sexually active, I never felt so valuable, so desired by people regardless of our skin.

When you are a gay boy of color growing up in America, it's hard to find images of your value in culture, let alone in yourself. You almost never see gay versions of yourself on mainstream TV. You're not in the porn, and when you are the thing is given some ridiculous title like *Django* and you are fetishized for your fat 280-inch black thick cut dick with a mushroom head that you use to pound on some poor, unprepared white twink. That or some different white guy is passed around a bunch of black/Latino guys in an orgy, servicing all those dicks, a flick with some creative title like "Black Dicks, White Ass." Pick whatever formula you want. In porn, black guys are virtually never shown as beautiful in the way that white guys almost always are. If you are black or Latino, you can be sure your race is animalized. If you are Asian, you can be sure to be feminized.

3

Beautiful white boys get to say hurtful things like "No Asians" or "Not into Black guys," or otherwise they speed straight to the point:

"Only into other white guys. I'm not racist. It's just a preference." Of course.

It's true that in gay online spaces, lots of colored boys say things like "no white dudes" or will specify that they are only into their own race, but that's not quite the same as when white guys say it. It doesn't have the same sting because white gay men are always in a position of power. You get the sense that brown bodies who are only into other brown bodies are creating communities for themselves and probably don't want to participate in anyone's dumb Django fantasies.

When we say that we're not into a certain group of people because it is "just a preference," we are lying to ourselves. The reality is that the great majority of our preferences, likes and desires are shaped by media and all the stuff we surround ourselves with. When the multi-billion dollar gay porn industry is 10,000% white dudes fucking other white frat bros, of course, you're going to think you're only attracted to other VGL hot masculine straight-acting white guys under the age of 30 with 2% body fat! It's not actually a preference at all — more like something you learn from all those years you've spent masturbating to porn. The media has everything to do with how we learn to relate to other people and how we perceive "others" more specifically.

Think about it for a second. It just doesn't make sense to say you are not attracted to an entire race of people. That's why I've always thought that when people say "I'm not attracted to X race," what they're actually telling you is that they're not attracted to the sensational way that particular race is framed by the media, the discursive image of that race that we see on TV. Brown boys all over have dated or had sex with at least one fine ass white boy who was like, "Wow, you are so unlike all the other black/Asian/brown/ Latino people I know."

The difficulty with talking about desire is that it's kind of a hopeless loop. I don't know why I'm primarily attracted to hipster, creative, artsy types of guys. It's just what I like. And that's the issue: we can all scream until we're blue in the face about gay racism. Every white gay dude in America who doesn't like black or brown guys can read this essay and it is not going to suddenly make them realize that they have been missing out all along. At the end of the day desire is personal and not even the best research results or compelling arguments can compete with "Well, it's what I like."

People just want to be normal. They want to be safe and earn a nice living, excel at the workplace and have a great life with somebody who is going to be there for them. Through sex and relationships, we bring people into our family, introduce them to our friends, invite them into our lives. We open ourselves up to our lovers and sometimes literally, your bottoms. That's why we go with what we know, what's safe, and why we have such trouble letting in anything that's going to make life difficult or weird.

There has to be a certain degree of similarity for any relationship to work. But I like when things are challenging. That's what makes life interesting.

10. THE TIME I OUTED MYSELF ON AIM

SHAWN BINDER | UPSTATE NEW YORK

THE FIRST TIME I smoked weed I was in my friend's bedroom during my freshman year of high school. We had grown up together and had become practically inseparable as she excelled beyond the rest of our peers in all things that, at the time, seemed adult and mature: boozing and boobs. She had developed early on in puberty while I was still waiting for armpit hair to grow in. She was sporting crop tops and bending older men to her will, while I was constantly being mistaken for a twelve-year-old. At restaurants, waitresses still asked if

I would like to see a kids' menu. And cashiers at the movie ticket booth always seemed skeptical when I requested a ticket to a PG-13 movie.

Fast forwarding into adulthood was an intoxicating idea, and I was determined to spend as much time with her as I could in the hopes that her maturity would rub off on me. She carried herself with an air of "I really don't give a fuck what you think because I listen to Bob Marley and skip school." She exuded a confidence that I could only dream of possessing.

After an unremarkable school day, I told my mom we would be going to my friend's house to do "homework." This usually was code for buying a pint of Ben & Jerry's and binge watching horror movies like *The Hills Have Eyes* or *House Of Wax* as we sipped cranberry vodkas, which were the only mixed drinks we knew how to make. My friend's house was always the best place to get into youthful trouble because while my parents would not allow me to bring a glass of water into the living room. She had a mother who seemed to have no problem giving free reign to a couple of fourteen-year-olds.

As we walked up to my friend's aging two-story house, a boy was leaning up against an old beige Honda Civic, smoking a Camel and biting his thumbnail. Now would probably be a good time to tell you all that I used the word "boy" loosely. In retrospect, this was a 20-year-old man. If I were a smarter 14-year-old, I would have realized just how creepy it was that a 20-year-old would hang out with 14-year-olds rather than spend his time masturbating or drinking PBR.

Recently, I looked him up on Facebook through some sleuthing and the only pictures he has available for public viewing are ones of him shirtless at some promotional event for a club. He looks surprisingly different than how he did back when I met him, but I imagine that's what aging and a ton of cocaine will do to one's body.

I'm not sure how my friend wound up meeting Erik. He was of medium height and had cropped light brown hair. He accentuated his sizable muscles and tattoos with a ribbed white tank top, which I thought was ridiculous even at the time. If life experience has taught me anything, it's that if you electively choose to wear a Hanes wife-beater and you're not a mechanic, you're not to be trusted. My instant sexual attraction to him was based purely off the fact that he had a penis and I had a penis — along with hidden desires to touch one that wasn't my own.

He finished smoking his cigarette and smiled a crooked smile. "How was school, kids?" Saying this with a wink. "It was good, real good!" I replied, my voice cracking slightly. Part of my fourteen-year-old self found being talked down to extremely sexy. It's one of those turn-ons that in retrospect I find confusing

My friend suggested we hang out in her room, and Erik nodded and threw his cigarette butt to the ground. We all walked into my friend's house and extracted a bottle of tequila from the booze cabinet. After closing the door to my friend's room, we began to gluttonously down shot after shot with no chaser, which made me feel like I had just sat through *Oldboy* entirely without flinching. After three shots apiece, Erik pulled out a small, rainbow-colored pipe from the book-bag he had slung over his shoulders.

Humming to himself, he began to pack something into it. When he was finished, he pulled out a lighter and handed the pipe to my friend. Taking a rip, she exhaled and let out a half-giggle, half-cough.

Erik motioned me over to where he sat with his index finger, and when I obliged, he pulled me toward himself. Whispering into my ear, he said, "You could be a model, you know that?" When you're 14 and in the closet and covered in bulbous pimples, kind words about your appearance can really cloud your sense of judgment. Mixed with the tequila, and flattered by a creep, I felt bold and sexual. "Hand me that pipe," I told my friend.

"Are you sure you can handle it?" she questioned.

"Yes, absolutely," I said, taking the pipe from Erik. He then held the lighter for me and instructed me on how to take all the smoke into my lungs. "Suck in hard, allow it to fill you up," he said.

"So I just put it to my mouth...and suck?" I asked him, trying to be seductive.

I put the pipe to my lips and nodded to him to light it. As instructed, I sucked in and took a deep breath. Immediately I began to violently cough and sputter. My throat felt like it had been lit on fire and no amount of deep breaths could quell the burn. At first I didn't feel anything besides the sharp stinging in my throat, but after a few minutes, my legs began to feel loose and my friend's tie-dye poster began to slowly swirl clockwise. I steadied myself against her desk proclaiming, "I need to eat, or I need to use the bathroom, I need..." The words seemed to stick in my throat.

"Here, I can show you where the bathroom is," Erik said. His eyes were glazed over but at the time I felt an electric shock pass between us. In retrospect, I was just stoned out of my mind. I had been to my friend's house on numerous occasions and knew exactly where her bathroom was, but I wasn't convinced in my ability to walk at the moment. I also wanted an excuse to get Erik alone. "Sure, yeah, can you show me?" I said.

He took my hand and led me down the hall, softly whispering into my ear, "You're going to be okay. It can be intense the first time. Don't panic." I thought his words were soothing and they kept my heart from feeling like it was about to burst out of my chest. As we reached the bathroom door, I stepped forward only to have him pull me back and hold me against his body. He began to rub my back, my butt, and my chest. "Um, I'll be right back," I said, pushing away from him and closing the bathroom door behind me.

Standing over the sink, I began splashing cold water on my face trying to sober up. What was going on? What was I doing? This was so uncharacteristic of me. I spent most of my time in school fighting off accusations about my sexuality, not getting high and letting boys rub me up and down. I need to pull it together, I told myself. I promised I would step out of the bathroom and tell him that I was straight and ask him not to touch me anymore because it made me uncomfortable. I had been slowly building up a facade of heterosexuality I projected to all my peers, and I would be damned if some man with a barbed wire arm tattoo was going to ruin that.

When I got out of the bathroom, he wasn't standing there like I had expected him to be. Instead I walked back into my friend's room to see the two of them sprawled on her bed, whispering and giggling to each other, as if trying to come to a consensus on something.

My friend looked up at me with a smirk that felt like she had been just let in on a dirty secret. "Well, I think I need to use the bathroom! Be right back!" she winked at me as she left, closing the door behind her with a slam. To this day, I don't think my friend was trying to set up a hook up between the two of us. I'd prefer to think that she left to get Pop-Tarts or something like that. My sexuality was never discussed during our friendship. However, I think she had her suspicions; anytime when we would hang out together, I would suggest we take the *Cosmo* sex surveys and ask her what it was like kissing men.

"C'mere," Erik said, rubbing the empty space next to him. He held up a shot glass, one in the shaped like a woman's rack, filled with tequila. "I poured it just for you." I took it from his hand and downed it, placing the glass down on the nightstand and slide next to him.

"You want to kiss me, don't you?" he said, pulling my boyish body towards his muscular, toned one. Without waiting for my answer, he shoved his mouth onto mine and began rubbing inside my thigh. At first I went along with it. I felt so mature, drinking liquor and making out with college-aged boys before I was even able to grow facial hair.

After a minute or so of being drowned by his tongue, I began to grow nervous. His hand kept lingering on my belt, playing with the skin between my belly button and the top of my jeans. This was all happening so fast. I was not ready for more than a peck and we had already escalated to the point where his tongue was practically punching my uvula. In a moment of clarity, I pushed him off of me seconds before my friend came back into the room. I like to think that even at that age, I had a level of self-preservation that has only come in handy once or twice in my life. Pushing a grown man off of me was probably one of these times.

"Did you two just kiss?" my friend asked us, smiling a smug little grin. "You look flustered." I immediately got up from the bed and announced that I needed to get home before dinner. Although my friend's house was a few miles from my own, I refused to call my mom and have her come to pick me up.

That night I cried myself to sleep. I felt so careless and stupid and stunted. Hours were spent rolling around in my bed, scenarios running through my head in which my classmates who taunted me day-in and day-out found about my alleged sexuality due about my brief moment with pot and penis.

The next day I signed onto AIM to a message from an acquaintance: "Heard what you did! ;)" I began to panic and profusely sweat immediately.

Fuck! Fuck! The jig is up. I'm caught, I'm fried, and I'm done. What will mom and dad think? What will my friends think? Ugh, what the fuck am I going to do? Think fast, you can back track, you can salvage this.

"I was just really drunk please don't tell anyone else I kissed him, I didn't want to it just of happened. Please promise me you won't tell anyone else." I sent back, hoping to inspire some sympathy from her. Instead I received the message, "Uh, I was talking about the pot…" before she signed off.

I spent the rest of the weekend pacing my room, biting my nails and wondering how quickly my AIM faux pas had traveled around the school. Growing up in Chester, New

York, I went to a school that consisted of 90 students per grade. Our school's mascot was Hambletonian, which I guess was the name of a "famous" racehorse from back in the day. From my extensive literary research, I found out that Hambletonian actually only won a single race in the entirety of his career. He did, however, father over 1000 other racehorses. If a daddy horse that peaked too early in life isn't the most perfect mascot for students who have little to do besides fornicate and smoke weed before class, then I don't know what is.

The thing about Chester was that the moment students decided to stick a label on you, it stuck for the rest of your time there. You were put with the same 90 students, and you would be with them for the next 13 years. I had been branded the "gay guy" long before I was even slightly sexually aware. I think it was because I preferred to spend my time with girls, passing our time putting milky pen makeup on beanie babies and playing elaborate games on the playground that strangely mirrored the plot of *Anaconda*. The way my classmates treated me, though, you would think I rolled through the halls on skates while wearing a crop top, throwing glitter into the air to the blaring soundtrack of *Hairspray*. This meant that they preferred to keep me at a safe distance at all times unless they were mocking me.

That Monday at school, as I walked through the hallway, heads slowly turned to snicker at me. "Faggot" bounced off the lockers between classes and one brazen boy even confronted me: "What's it like kissing another dude? You homo!" I quickly discovered that my admittance hadn't just been over instant message to one person; the entire school had been informed. I had spent years getting angry and denying rumors about my sexuality because I was afraid to let them all know they might have been right in sensing there was something different about me. However, through one afternoon of debauchery and a single AIM conversation, I had outed myself to the entire school.

My close friends did not react in any negative way to the rumors circulating that day, and instead chose to fill our conversations with more pressing matters: television and online video games. Although my other friends were wonderful, I avoided the particular friend with whom I had partied. When she came to sit with us at the lunch table, I remember excusing myself from the cafeteria and heading out of school through the back door. There was a wooded area that ran along the edge of the building where I always imagined horny teenagers would give each other hand jobs after class. It was here that I cut through the trees, determined to walk the three miles home. I remember being angry, the kind of angry that makes you want to throw up just so you can get the rage out. I remember screaming into the deep woods as I trekked back to my house.

Eventually I had to stop faking head colds to miss school. My parents unknowingly sent me back to school so that I had to face all my peers for whole days at a time. At first, people continued their whispers, but then, in typical high school fashion, everyone moved on. I spent those two weeks denying what had happened to anyone brazen enough to ask me. People grew bored with my refusal to acknowledge their insults and went back to sniffing glue sticks. On occasion I would be taunted on the bus or told to turn around in the locker room because boys were worried about undressing in front of me. But after those two weeks, the taunting seemed to hurt me significantly less.

I would out myself online again when accidentally copying and pasting a MySpace survey and forgetting to change the answer to the question "What are your interests?" from the previous girl's answer of "pink, shopping, and boys!"

At the time, I thought these incidents would ruin my life. I thought they would completely destroy my relationships with friends and family and that I would be cast out. When you're in high school the mistake of divulging information to the wrong person can seem disastrous. I spent countless hours in my bed, my stomach aching with worry because I was afraid of someone finding out about my sexuality.

Back then being a homosexual was something that I had not even begun to fully understand. Now that I'm older, I'm not afraid of sharing those things anymore because I'm slowly learning to be comfortable with every part of my identity, even the most revealing parts. I used to be afraid of holding a boy's hand in public, the jeers of my past coming back to me in waves. But I'm not afraid anymore, and that lack of fear feels like a satisfying middle finger in the air.

11. MUCH ADO ABOUT A NAME

MAR CURRAN | CHICAGO

I HAVE BEEN DREADING my graduation for months.

No one really knows this, of course. I'm not one to play the martyr, and my flippant facade of aloofness to mimic *The L Word*'s Shane is pretty crucial to my identity at this point. It is hard being 22 and feeling awkward, so I pretend I don't. Mar, he had that one huge party where people got down to their underwear and danced, or that one where Nate threw up in a bucket on the couch and Mar didn't even freak out, isn't he a great guy? Mar, he came out as trans* and is the president of the queer group on campus, he knows people, didn't you hear? Mar, he hangs out with people in their late twenties and they all organize together and he's respected by important people, do you know him? Not: Mar, he might cry if he goes on stage and someone says his birth name in front of an audience who knows better. Being 22 and trying to be seen as cool takes maintaining an image.

So I've been shaking off people's questions, lying about possibly just skipping it to brunch with some friends or work on a piece for the queer website I write for. There's just so much important work to do, I scoff, I don't have time to sit through a ceremony. Inside, I am squirming under bright lights while everyone asks why that guy has a girl's name as he walks across the stage.

I shaved my face this morning. I'm no good at it, so it's still covered in stubble and itches. It's not really my fault that I never had that Hallmark bonding moment of my dad teaching me to shave. The only time we've ever discussed it is when I come home and it's done poorly, he will raise his voice while brushing the sides of his face, fuming, "This? Needs to be gone next time. Got it?" I always roll my eyes and nod. South Side Irish Catholic families are not known for bonding over deep emotional discussions.

I am wearing a new button-down shirt and conservative tie, my oversized men's khakis, shiny black patent-leather shoes. My hair is combed back, and I have my fanciest pair of glasses on. I smell of Old Spice deodorant and anxiety sweats, a perfect combination to appease my parents while simultaneously conveying everyone with any level of perception that I do not want to be there. The overpriced cap and gown fit nicely into a plastic bag I can dispose of at my university's stadium where I will be on display. I sigh.

A professor once told me graduations aren't actually about the graduate. They're about the people who supported the graduate to get to this place in life and celebrating themselves. I know this is exactly how my parents feel, because I once told my mother this story and she just tilted up her chin and said, "That's true." Every time I have brought up skipping my graduation, she uses her stern voice. She calls me my birth name with lips pulled in tightly as, a thin, line forms across her face. I am a perfect amalgamation of my parents' faces, so it's like Future Me is glaring right at me in any given moment around them, which is disconcerting. I actually play out conversations between myself at different timeline points in my head when reassuring myself that I haven't totally fucked up my life, so my mother personifying that can be a bit much to handle.

Somehow they talked me into being here.

I have never liked ceremonies, as far as I know. I remember crying about how itchy my dress was at my South Side Irish Catholic First Holy Communion, which is a lot of capital letters, but if you identify with some combination of those words, you know that's just how it is. My Confirmation ended with me crying because I was so frustrated with the number of photographs my parents wanted to take. I think I lasted half an hour in my high school graduation dress before I started complaining about how I couldn't breathe in it. To be fair, my school required every girl to wear wedding dresses to graduation, and those are not known for their comfort.

The common theme here, though, is that I ended up at those ceremonies, too, and as an older and less angry Mar knows, sometimes it's better to just not waste time fighting my parents.

I get to the stadium on time before realizing I don't know where to check in. I fidget in place, pretending to check my phone until I see someone I know and ask them where to go. I should have gotten a minor in Social Avoidance — but it's too late for that at this point, I think. I rush to an auditorium with smiling staff behind banquet tables, handing sheets of paper to my peers. I stumble up to the appropriate middle-aged woman.

"Name?" I blush and tell her my birth name, scanning the room for odd stares but am met with the realization that on graduation day people really only give a shit about themselves and getting across that stage so they're done with school already. I am relieved.

I turn to find her fumbling through long lists, brows furrowed. "I don't see that name here. Could it be under something else?" The air is siphoned from my lungs. Did I register to graduate incorrectly, and now I won't be able to matriculate? Did I not graduate at all? How do I tell my parents, grandparents, and teen sister, all waiting in the stands for me? Will this be listed as another one of my irresponsible yet endearing mistakes, or was I going to be in some sort of trouble for this? How much trouble can a 22-year-old get into with his parents who he receives no financial assistance from and hasn't lived with in over three years? Would they still take me out to dinner as planned if I didn't go through the diploma dance here today?

It couldn't be under any other name. Right?

"Can you check under 'Mar Curran?'" I venture, timid and tripping over my words. She shuffles the stack again. "We have a ... here." She reads my chosen name.

I had done the request for graduation one October evening, a beer by my side, cross-legged on my grimy futon. My resolute scowl was reflected back to me in the dim laptop screen: "Please enter your name as listed on your legal documents." I entered my chosen full name. A red line of text appeared, brandished above my apparent error to shame me. No, what's your REAL name, weirdo. I closed the window. I returned the next morning, sober and defeated, resubmitting with my birth name on the page.

Application Accepted.

But now I am here, wearing a tie and knees weak, and I am being told that I am in effect having my biggest Coming Out yet.

I am not prepared for this. I have been psyching myself up for the mortifying defeat of being announced as my birth name for weeks, yes, but I did not plan to come out to my grandparents this way so that stone cold fear is a new slap in the face. You know those funny stories we all tell each other, about the worst coming out story we've ever heard? The old myth of telling your parents you are dying, pulling the rug out from under them with, "Just kidding, I'm gay." My mom once asked me if I was gay while driving on Lake Shore Drive, and I remembered stories of parents wrecking cars like queerness wrecked their dreams for their children's lives. I take a deep breath.

"Is that not your name?" All of the blood in my body is racing to my face and I blurt out, "That's not the name my parents will be expecting to be called onstage." "Well," she says, laying her papers down in front of herself, "What do you want to be called?"

This is one of my favorite questions supportive people ask when they figure out something's going on, like how excited I get when someone asks my pronoun preference. After over twenty years of never getting asked something so basic and intrinsic to who you are, it always brings a wave of warmth to me. I tell her my name.

Five minutes later, I am outside frantically texting my parents and sister. "They didn't use my birth name. I'm not sure how it happened. Just tell Nana it's a typo or something — that there's another kid with the same last name and they put his name in here. I didn't know about it." My sister texts back that my parents are pissed. I am surprisingly not upset about that. I don't feel guilt over their denial and what I see as the Universe (with a capital U, yes) giving them the side-eye and me a pat on the back.

I take my seat. I am sitting near an acquaintance from my freshman year, but otherwise a sea of strangers surrounds me. The repulsion of ceremonies I usually wear like a badge of honor does not sweep across my face. To be frank, it's been replaced by giddiness and glee. They put my real name in the booklet! And they're going to call me my real name when I got my diploma! Will it be on my diploma too? Now my parents have seen my real name! I am grinning.

Speakers rise, pontificate on the job market and finding oneself, sit back down, one after another. I cannot help but notice that my usual Catholic guilt, sitting like a sewer system in my abdomen, is not activating. Having my name be in my hands, for what feels like one of the only times it truly has been, has made me euphoric. I am nervous, excited, exuberant, sitting with sweaty palms, feeling almost religious about my name appearing on paper for all to see.

My row stands. Ian is sitting with the band. He is one of my closest queer friends, a member of my "gamily" (a term that's a mash-up of gay and family). He is always telling me what an inspiration I am to him. Today, when I look into his eyes as they call out "Mar Curran," I actually believe him. His cheering is the only one I can hear.

I meet my family after the ceremony. I am fumbling, drunk on the moment, basking in the knowledge that no one will bring up that my birth name was not called out in order to maintain polite conversation. I hug my grandparents. My sister raises her eyebrows at me and whispers, "Good job." We take photos together, like good families do at these sorts of things. My dad gives me his patented "I'm Your Dad and I'm About To Scold You" look. "That wasn't the name I wanted read," he mutters, or something to that effect; the message is clearly conveyed. Birth name or nothin'. Even having "Mar" called out is offensive to his lifestyle, though he has only started disliking the nickname he himself used for me as a child since I have used it as my genderless moniker of choice. His hands are on his hips and his lips are pursed. I let out a light laugh and tell him it's one of my compromises. We stay silent and look off in the distance.

He sits to my left. Dinner is tense for a while. I am trying not to provoke my father but my boisterous energy is unrelenting; I am visibly happier than I have been for weeks. Usually this is something to suppress; my father is a man who likes his calm meals, quiet TV watching, silent drives with the radio humming. Calm, quiet, silent. I exemplify the moments I love most about my father; gregarious and laughing, telling stories and making pithy remarks to amuse his audience. The best parts of me are from him. I am a performer at heart, making small quips and engaging in detailed stories with others. These are the parts that annoy of me I always feel rub him the exact wrong way. I used to hate these parts but now see them as our shared lineage, proof that we did indeed get cut from the same cloth, even if I'm just some gay scraps. I'll never understand why he hates these parts that remind me of him. I order a beer I know will get me tipsy quickly, a local microbrew that costs twice as much as I'd spend on myself. I'm celebrating, even if no one else feels like it now.

We all discuss our order choices. The group gets input into my sister's choice of chicken, whether my mother will like the pasta, if I should order two eggplant parmesan sandwiches so I can eat one tomorrow for lunch. Dad mentions getting a calzone. "That crap will give you a heart attack tonight if you eat that," I scoff at him, looser with alcohol, braver with defiance. There is a pause in table talk, and I loom up from my menu to see him trying not to laugh. "Well, something's going to give me a heart attack tonight," he says. I smile.

I keep the booklet with my real name in it safely tucked away under my bed. I haven't discussed my name with my family since I put it away that night.

12. THE COUPLE UNDERCOVER

OSCAR RAYMUNDO | NEW YORK, NEW YORK

I GRABBED ALL THE papers and stuffed them in the glossy navy blue folder they gave me at the orientation an hour earlier. My hotel room was spacious in the color of cream but nothing I'd brag about. I had a great view of 7th Avenue. New York was misty that day. I scrambled to the restroom, fixed my hair and picked up the small bottle of Burberry cologne I bought just for the occasion. I sprayed it a few inches in front of me and forced my way right into the floating fragrance, feeling the small particles land on my blazer and on my lime green tie. The tie matched my Kenneth

Cole watch. While admiring my watch, I caught a glimpse of the time. I was already late for the first meeting. I rushed out my room and down to the lobby to the main conference room.

The room was crowded with college boys all wearing black blazers. I walked in with confidence, a trait I was certain we all shared. Minutes before anyone ascended to the podium, I took a seat towards the back, the perfect location for scoping out the entire room. I opened my folder. The first thing on the itinerary of this two-day networking conference in the heart of New York for overachieving, Ivy League-educated gay undergrads was welcoming remarks from some hotshot at Lehman Brothers.

Like most of my misadventures, it all began with innocent flirtation. I first heard of the conference two months earlier from a handsome, raven-haired Columbia boy I met at a dive bar in the East Village. He bragged that the conference was a great opportunity to meet recruiters, network around and hopefully land that golden ticket of an internship at one of the big banks. While he had intentions of becoming a high rolling banker, I had intentions of marrying one. That night, drunk and with smeared in ambitions, I crafted a new resume, highlighting my short-lived gig at a business magazine and exaggerating my desire to enroll in an MBA program. I lied, applied and got in.

Dozens of well put-together young gay men vying to be one step ahead in the competitive world of finance and then there was me, overcrowded public school, waitlisted at Princeton, dismal G.P.A., creative writing major me. A guy with dirty blond hair raised his hand to ask the first question. Initiative, I liked that. Two minutes later, he raised it again to ask another question. Then another. Eagerness was not so flattering. My eyes met those of an intelligent-looking boy off to my right. He had tied his tie in an Onassis knot, so he didn't retain my interest for long. The guy sitting right in front of me was wearing pounds of hair product. This was going to take longer than I thought.

Next item on the itinerary, we are asked to break up into small groups, and we're given a business problem. We're expected to work together and come up with a profitable solution to a hypothetical dilemma involving the merging of two fast food chains. Bottom line: who gives a shit? Instead I volunteered to be the note-taker in my group and silently agreed to absolutely everything this Yale undergrad, who imposed his leadership on the rest of us, had to say. The best way to deal with an Ivy Leaguer was to pretend he was always correct.

The post-dinner plan that first night was a casual cocktail hour. Basically, another excuse for more handshakes and more smiles, just as self-congratulatory as courtesy blowjobs sans an orgasm. The real enticing thing was the bite of hot gossip I had swallowed during dinner. According to a petite pretty boy from Stanford, the year before all of the guys at the conference had gotten utterly wasted and somehow ended up at one of the organizer's West Village townhouse engaging in questionable behavior. To evade further controversy this year, you had to wear a special red sticker on your name tag in order to get alcoholic beverages. Only the organizers had them.

After my second Diet Coke, I couldn't bear the dry spell any longer. The only thing worse than being forced to make small talk with men in J. Crew was doing it completely sober. In the restroom, I noticed that one of the organizers had forgotten his name tag next to the sink, the name tag with the red sticker! Cautious not to get caught, I grabbed the tag and dashed inside a stall. I slowly peeled the red sticker from the organizer's tag and stuck it right on mine. After smoothing it out a bit, I left the restroom and headed towards the bar to order a glass with ice and gin. Waiting behind me in line, the pretty kid from Stanford did a quick double take, noticed my red sticker and asked, "How did you get that?"

"I stole it," I responded without guilt.

"Well, someone is getting started early," he said.

"Aren't you?" I questioned, raising my eyebrow down at him, just a few inches shorter than me.

"I'm saving myself," he said, slipping a small piece of paper the size of a Chinese fortune into my fingers.

"What is this?"

"An address in the West Village. Do you want to come? The guy who lives there, he works for Boston Consulting, and I heard he is looking for guys to accompany him to Paris later this month. Can you believe it?"

*****

From the foyer of the West Village townhouse, I could see two chandeliers and listen to the crackling of a gentle fireplace. Men in suits paced around, mingling while balancing bubbly champagne glasses filled halfway to the rim. The living room bathed in amber. Across the hall, I ran into the

Columbia student who had originally told me about the conference.

"You made it!" He gave me a hug, and I could smell the whiskey.

"I did," I smiled.

"Isn't it grand? I can see myself finding a hookup here."

"Oh, are there a lot of single guys here?" I sounded way too enthused.

"No, I meant, offers. But if you're interested I hear some guys are playing strip poker upstairs."

"Really?"

"No," Columbia laughed grossly. "Fire Island is that way!" He snapped his finger to my left.

"Actually, it's behind you." I excused myself to the kitchen and poured myself a glass of Dom. I strolled into the piano room where an unknown pianist played a harmless

"Oh, I'm sorry. You don't look Mexican."

I squinted my eyes, offended.

"Please, I don't subscribe to identity politics, we all know that," he motioned towards his two compatriots who nodded briefly and looked back towards me for my response.

"To answer your question melody in the background. There I overheard the guy from Yale discussing the economy with two other students. He seemed to think that the decibel level of his voice somehow played into the effectiveness of his argument.

"You're from Spain," he said as soon as I got near. "How do you think you should we fix Europe?"

"I'm Mexican," my words came out like buzzkill.

"Oh, I'm sorry. You don't look Mexican."

I squinted my eyes, offended.

"Please, I don't subscribe to identity politics. We all know that," he motioned towards his two compatriots who nodded briefly and looked back towards me for my response.

"To answer your question, about Europe," I reverted, for I did have an opinion on the matter, "we have to recognize the limits of capitalism."

"Not this crap again!" Yale interrupted.

"He's right," your soothing voice trailed in from behind me. "We were too optimistic about the Euro," you said.

"Yeah, but blaming capitalism? How passé," Yale blurted. "People need incentives."

"In the form of million dollar bonuses?" You asked.

"Whatever. Got any more coke?" Yale asked his friend, as they began to walk away. But then Yale, desperate to have the final word, stopped and turned back at us. "I'd just be careful about your dissidence. Your drink was probably paid for by a bonus."

We didn't respond back. I was just excited to be in your company.

"Thanks so much for that," I smiled at you. "I felt like I walked right into the lion's den."

"Don't worry about it," you said. "They're harmless. And you had a point. As socialist as it might have been."

"There's nothing wrong with socialism," I defended myself.

"You are too trusting."

"Maybe."

"Where do you go to school?" you asked. It was the first time at the conference anyone had taken an interest in anything beyond themselves.

"I'm living in the city this summer, but I go to school in Chicago."

"University of Chicago? That's a great school."

"Northwestern."

"That's an even better school," you smiled and kept your mouth open so that you could quickly steal a sip from my drink.

"You know there is an entire bar next to the kitchen," I said teasingly.

"I just wanted to know what you were drinking," you said and flashed a twinkled smile.

"You could always ask."

You then told me your name and that you were about to start your senior year at Princeton. Your family lived in the Upper East Side so just like the guys from Columbia and NYU, you were not staying at the hotel with the rest of us. You had just gotten back from studying abroad in Argentina. You really had no interest in being an investment banker, but your father, a principal at McKinsey, forced you to come.

"I want to work for a non-profit," you continued.

I looked at you in silence, almost in awe, realizing how I never considered that a selfless heart should also be a must-have in a mate. Before you could really notice my idolizing stare, your phone vibrates.

"Listen, my dealer's downstairs, would you like to find a room upstairs and smoke a joint with me?" And just like that, I found myself smoking pot with a nice, down-to-earth Princeton boy whose dreams of helping the world outweighed the desire to stuff his wallet. We snuck upstairs and found an empty bedroom with a large window leading out to the fire escape. I turned on the desk lamp and took my coat off. You took off yours, and we both tossed them neatly on the bed. Together we huddled on the ledge by the open window and lit your poorly rolled joint. As I took a hit, I envisioned my future life with this trophy of a man.

Inhale.

Your parents, progressive and supportive, would find me a breath of fresh air in their stuffy Upper East Side existence. I'd delight the sophisticates at the galas and fundraisers and they'd be okay with me staying at home writing in my underwear while you worked. Every morning before another draining day at the office, I'd have your coffee ready just the way you like it, foamy and brown. During the day, I'd take our dog, a husky named London, out for a walk around Central Park and have dinner reservations made before you got home. I'd iron your shirts, your ties and give you foot rubs on the weekends while our cat, Vienna, purrs indulgently by our side. We'd live below 14th Street because you'd never be able to prevent me from being hip. And you'd say to all your friends that was what you loved most about me.

"Why are you looking at me that way?" you asked, suddenly self-aware, taking the joint from my sticky fingers.

"Because you're gorgeous," I said. Your head dropped with grace, and I could tell you were blushing. I placed my hand on your shoulder and leaned in, eyes closed, lips perched, desiring to kiss you. But I never reached your mouth. I opened my eyes and instead you retracted away from me, your hand clutching on to my forearm, barricading me from moving in any further.

"Is there something wrong?" I asked, confused, unsure of what to do with this great sudden need to be close to you.

"I'm sorry," you sprung up from the ledge and began to pace frantically around the empty room. "I can't believe I'm actually doing this. It's not at all what you think."

"I don't know what to think."

"I'm straight."

I shrugged, "I'm a socialist."

"There aren't opportunities for straight white guys, you know? I can't pretend to be black but I can pretend to…"

"Show interest in me?" I asked. "Well, you wouldn't be the first guy to ever do that."

"I thought I'd flirt a little, get a couple of business cards in my pocket and be home by midnight," you explained yourself. "But then I started getting drilled down there. The gay Ivy-Leaguers, they have like a secret lingo or something I just couldn't seem to decipher. I'd figure it'd be best if I just..."

"Hid out upstairs and got high?"

"Listen, I liked hanging out with you. I shouldn't have given you the wrong idea."

"Don't worry, your secret's safe with me. I'm not going to out you to Boston Consulting."

"Thank you."

"And since we're being completely honest, I'm not really here trying to break into banking anyway. I'm secretly scoping out potential husbands," I stood up and walked towards the bed to get my coat.

"That's not very socialist of you. Going through all this just to find a sugar daddy?" You sound rather disappointed, as if somehow you expected more from me. But this was it. This was my master plan.

"I don't expect you to understand," I said putting on my coat.

"Don't you have any aspirations?" Your tone went from bewildered to mildly insulting.

"I want to be a writer," I said, leveling up my defenses. "I'm just not fully prepared to starve in some shithole on the Lower East Side for the rest of my life."

"And marrying for money is your solution? It just sounds to me like you're not giving yourself enough credit. I mean, have you even tried?"

I refused to answer your condescending question. All I knew how to do was try.

"Congratulations. I'm sure you'll make a great banker: deceptive, scheming and controlling, ready to pounce on a sure thing. Daddy will be proud," I stopped talking and made my way towards the door, choosing not to fight for a trophy husband custom built for someone else's mantle.

"Don't be like that," you said. "I just think you are so much better than that."

"You don't know anything about me," I said.

"I know that you're smart. And that you go to an awesome school. You're goddamn determined." After a second you finished with, "Unfortunately, I can't speak as to your kissing skills." You then flashed your devil teeth.

"Well, thanks for being honest," I said calmly.

"Ah, I thought I was deceptive," you tried to keep fighting, but I could tell it was just for fun.

"Out there," I pointed towards the door, with the rest of the bankers, the college students, the interns and the prodigal sons, "out there you are one hell of a liar. In here, I'm glad we're being honest."

"How am I going to get out of here in one piece?" you asked, weighing your exit strategies.

"With another lie and a liar on your side," I suggested and grabbed you by the arm. The doors of the bedroom flung open and you and I walked out. We graced our way down the stairs and through the hallway on the first floor. Some of the men in the living room took notice of our early departure and watched. You and I made the perfect couple. The power couple. The champagne toast couple. The sailing in the Greek isles couple. The couple you'd kill to have at your house for dinner. The couple you'd die to have in your bed for a threesome. The proud yet pleasant couple. At the door, you grabbed my face quickly and kissed me with our mouths closed.

"What was that all about?" I whispered as my cheeks turned to scarlet.

"We want to make this believable right?"

Outside on the front steps, you shook my hand, gave me your business card, wished me good luck, said goodbye, headed out to look for a cab and disappeared forever. I was left alone with enough time for reality to fade back in. I realized we weren't perfect. My perfect husband would have hugged me, kissed me and never let me go. He would love me unconditionally until the end of time.

Exhale.

13. MY HIDEOUS ANGEL

Randall Jenson | St. Louis, Missouri

THE SUMMER AFTER MY sophomore year of college, I met a wonderful woman, a community activist who allowed me the nonjudgmental space to first start to share with her parts of my story about growing up in an abusive home, coming out as gay and being homeless. It was the first real opportunity I was presented with to truly reflect on my journey of emerging out of violence and moving past survival mode. I will always be grateful to her for believing me.

Our conversations ended up as the core story of the main stage production of *The*

Home Project by About Face Youth Theatre in 2006. It premiered at Victory Gardens Theatre during the same summer that the Gay Games were hosted in Chicago. The show opened with the following lines, which I'd uttered to my friend during our initial conversation: "It's time to go. I'm leaving St. Louis. I'm leaving these streets, these rusting benches, these allies, this park, my family. St. Louis is always going to be one of those places in my life that I'll only visit if I have to, and I won't stay long. Too much has happened here...."

*****

I attended my first grade school in historic St. Charles, Mo. It was a private academy, nestled on the edge of the Missouri River, where all the students wore crisp white-and-navy uniforms. The academy had nuns in black habits with stinky-cotton-ball breath, and we even learned that a Catholic saint was buried on our school grounds. During my primary year my homeroom teacher asked all the students to draw a picture of our families for an upcoming parent-teacher night. I remember creating a detailed family portrait as a cassette tape of *The Little Mermaid* played in the background. In the picture I was the skinny, happy little boy standing between my two parents. I was holding their hands. My smiling Mexican mom, only 5 feet tall, had a bobble head full of dark, curly hair. My tall white dad wore thick glasses and towered over all of us with his 6-foot stature. While my mom also held on to a purse, my dad held on to a brown paper bag with a bottle inside it.

Unfortunately, these last two illustrative details made my teachers suspicious about what else might be happening at home. I remember answering a myriad of questions about my dad. I innocently answered that, yes, my dad almost always had a bottle or can in his hand, and yes, my dad would drink from this nightly. Well, my mom was then called into a meeting. I remember how embarrassed she looked. I didn't yet understand that we were a working-class family. We were already considered different by those around us. My parents would tell me that it was a "privilege" to be "accepted" into this prestigious academy. On top of this, my family was multiracial. I quickly learned how to stay silent. Regrettably, I learned from my parents that what others thought about us mattered the most.

My mom initially denied my drawings. She explained to teachers that I'd drawn those details for attention, even though I didn't know that drawing a brown bag in my dad's hand was attention-worthy. She learned how to excuse my "acting out" when I started to tell teachers at my school about the arguments I saw at home. Everything culminated in a finale the following year.

During lunchtime in the cafeteria, I flung a ketchup packet at my best friend, Adam, and it landed in his hair. I'm not really sure why I did this. Maybe I was trying to appear cool? Maybe I was influenced by my childhood idol and first crush, Kevin Arnold from *The Wonder Years*, who performed a similar incident to impress Winnie Cooper in the pilot episode of the show? All I know is that I was asked to leave the academy.

As I grew older, my mom often reminded me that I was dismissed from this private academy. I was reminded that my actions were a direct source of shame for my family. I internalized a variety of messages from my parents telling me that I was a liar. I learned that no one would believe me when I told adults about what was going on at home. Indeed, I learned very quickly that "what happens in the family should stay in the family."

*****

By the time I was 9 years old, my parents' marriage was quickly unraveling. My dad would spend his time away on week-long business trips and leave me, my mom and my new baby sister to ourselves. I was forced to switch schools; my second Catholic grade school was in the rural town of Wentzville, Mo. Many of the students were from working-class Irish, German and Italian families. However, almost the entire student body was still white, and many of their parents quickly decided that my mom's tanner skin tone and our family's dysfunction were reason enough to keep their children away from me.

Lunchtime was a highlight of the school day. I would often sit alone and not socialize with my peers, finding solace in introversion. As I grew more aware of my father's violence and alcoholism, I coped with these realities by eating through second and third helpings of lunchtime Sloppy Joes and baked potatoes. I quickly became known as a chubby, unathletic, sensitive boy from a bad home.

At school we attended mass every Wednesday morning. Every week we had religion classes. We learned about Catholic spirituality, and every so often we touched on human sexuality, but we never discussed gay people, aside from the occasional reminders at church that we should "love the sinner, hate the sin." At home I certainly didn't learn anything positive about what it means to be gay. Still, my romantic crushes blossomed. In the summer of 1993, at 10 years old, I fell in love with the movie *Free Willy*. Well, more specifically, I fell in love with Jesse, the rebellious teenager who is the main character in *Free Willy*. In the movie Jesse escapes homelessness and the foster-care system. He is even able to find a family (and a whale) that love him back. I was growing up. I had moved on from the middle-school Kevin Arnolds of this world, and it couldn't have been more perfect.

That September my baby brother was born. My sister was now 3 years old, and our family was a full house. My dad was still very absent from our home at this point, and when he did return home on weekends, he was most often drunk. If he was in a good mood, he'd playfully wrestle with me and give my sister piggyback rides around our house, ignoring my mom. If he was angry, he'd argue with and yell at my mom. The first time I saw my dad hit my mom, I was standing at the top of our stairs. I stared through the wooden railings as my dad's hand slapped my mom across the face and she fell into our foyer's door. I will never forget those images.

I remember my parents' final fight. My dad, in an attempt to further scare my mom, threatened to kill her father. He called my grandpa a "dirty old Spic." My mom yelled something back, but I can't even recall what she said, because the next thing I saw was my dad punching my mom. She screamed and fell to the floor. He then dragged my mom across our living-room carpet by her hair, leaving her face scraped, her legs bruised and her body bloody. At 10 years old I jumped on him with all my might to try and get him off my mom. He hurled me off him and into our living-room wall. At this point in their marriage, we had 911 on speed dial. The police arrived yet again, answering a call about a "domestic dispute." I'm not entirely sure why, but this time they seemed to understand the extent of our abuse. They finally took my dad away, and he never spent another night in our home.

After this my dad filed for divorce and was able to have the hearings held in the small, rural, Mayberryesque town where he lived. He had been secretly claiming residence there for the past year. My ethnically ambiguous mom was screwed over in the divorce proceedings and lost most of her assets. A year and a half later we even lost the home that she had purchased with her entire savings. We spent a week living in a Super 8 Hotel, temporarily homeless, since my dad had failed to pay the monthly mortgage dictated by the divorce decree.

There was one positive thing that came out of their divorce. During the hearings I was called into the court by the judge to give a short testimony about the violence I had endured at the hands of my dad. Though the judge granted my dad regular visitation rights with my two younger siblings, because of the extent of my abuse, he did not force me to see my dad.

After my parents' divorce was finalized, I spent a lot of time helping watch my younger brother and sister. My mom was now a single parent and tried her best to give her three children a private-school education. I became the primary caretaker for my siblings and tried to be a good older brother to them. One Christmas my mom gave my little sister a small amount of shopping money, which she spent on gifts from the flea market behind our church. When I unwrapped my gift, I saw a hideous ceramic cherub staring up at me. My sister asked if I liked it. Of course I said yes, trying my best to be gracious. Still, I thought,

"What the hell am I going to do with this?" I quickly put it up on my dresser, and it always stayed there, collecting dust and staying out of the way, far from most of my things.

For three years I attended a private, Catholic, all-boys high school where I excelled as debate captain. I was involved in anything that wasn't sports, because I still sucked at sports. I learned to accept that I am gay and push past the initial fears that I was going to hell. I figured that if God made everyone in his own image and likeness, then I must be pretty intentional. I managed to make a few close friends and started to spend weekend nights at different friends' houses. This provided me with an escape, since things were becoming tenser at home all the time. I wish that I could say that things got better at home during my teenage years, but they didn't.

Even though my dad was out of the picture, my mom refused to seek family counseling for all of us. She spiraled into depression, anger and rage. She became very physically violent toward my siblings and me. I struggled with how much I could share about my family with my peers, their parents and my teachers. I was still being told not to talk about what happened at home. When my mom would try to slap me during an argument, I would often flinch before her hand hit my face. For every flinch she would add an extra slap. She teased me, reminding me that a real man would "stand and take it." She would insult my femininity, grab my fat and imply that I was really a girl because I had a chubby chest.

I received the brunt of the abuse in my teenage years. By the time I came out to her as gay at 16 years old, we were in an all-out war at home. During arguments she would chase me around our small apartment with any object she could find: a cordless telephone, a metal pan, a high-heeled shoe. She would hit me to the door and then start to kick me out. After a while I just gave up on trying to fight back, and when she told me to leave, I simply would.

What began as a few hours outside the home turned into a few days, and before long I had missed too many weeks at school as well, so I was kicked out of my high school. During all this I ended up trying yet again to commit suicide and entered into a children's psychiatric unit. After I was released my mom kicked me out again. I was now homeless.

*****

In the summer of 2001, I was 17 years old and staying in a youth emergency shelter. While there I met a graduate student in social work who was volunteering at the shelter. She showed an interest in me, and one evening she broke the agency's rules and snuck me out, taking me to Growing American Youth, the local lesbian, gay, bisexual, transgender and queer group located in the gay-friendly neighborhood of the Central West End. It was my first time being around other LGBTQ youth, and I was terrified.

I shared with the youth group leader what was happening to me at home, revealing that I was scared and homeless. The youth leader asked me to share my story with the other youth in the group. Since there were few spaces for LGBTQ youth to go, there were over 60 youth at this meeting. After I told my story the youth leader asked everyone, "How many of you, at some point or another, have been kicked out for being gay?" I remember over half the kids raising their hands. That was over 30 youth!

I remember thinking how crazy this was. I couldn't believe that this was happening. I couldn't accept that this was normal. It seemed to be such an institutional issue, such an expected journey for me and my peers simply because we were queer. This was the moment that sparked my passion for activism. After the meeting a few members of the youth group came up to me and told me about places where I could stay. I decided to go with the safest option, one that would allow me to try to finish high school.

Legally, I could stay in the shelter for up to two weeks before my mom would be reported to the Division of Family Services. It felt unreal that the staff knew that my mom would kick me out again but couldn't immediately report her. It was only if she failed to pick me up from the shelter that they could do so. Their hands were tied. When my mom was forced to pick me up from the shelter, she angrily informed me that I shouldn't expect to stay in the apartment for long. She told me that I was going to be kicked out again. The next day, when my mom left for work, I went into the small bedroom that my brother, my sister and I shared. I quickly packed up everything I could find. I tore my X-Men posters off the wall, gathered up my clothes and organized a memory box full of childhood stuff.

It was the end of summer and right before school was to begin. My brother and sister were out in the living room, watching *Gullah Gullah Island* and *Blue's Clues.* I remember calling them into the bedroom and explaining to them that I was leaving. I had to go. When my sister asked why, I shared, "Remember how Mom always kicks me out of the house and calls me a faggot and stuff?"

"What's a faggot?" my brother asked innocently.

"Well, it's a really bad word," I replied, "but what it means is 'gay.'"

My sister followed up asking, "Well, what's 'gay'?"

"Well, instead of you liking Tommy in your class, it would mean you like Becky," I explained. "So it's when a boy likes a boy, or when a girl likes a girl. Well, I'm gay."

They both looked at me and said, quite simply, "That's OK." We all started hugging and crying.

When I was getting ready to leave, my sister looked up at my dresser, pointed and said, "You forgot your angel."

I quickly replied, "I know. I know. I just have so much stuff--"

"You have to take it," she interrupted. "It will watch over you."

I moved around a lot after I left home. I lived with different friends and their families before graduating from my second high school, a public school in St. Louis. I had to repeat my junior year, since I didn't have enough credits from my first high school, but in the spring of 2003, I received a full scholarship to DePaul University.

*****

After living in Chicago for almost 10 years, I recently moved back to St. Louis, accepting the LGBTQ Youth Advocate position at Safe Connections, a local anti-violence organization. This position is the first paid position in the St. Louis region geared toward helping change the culture and climate surrounding LGBTQ youth in schools, youth-serving spaces and community agencies, and I am honored to be doing this work. It has been over 12 years since I initially packed my bags and left home at 17, and it feels like I've come full circle.

Through my activism I've often had the privilege of speaking to a variety of LGBTQ young people over the years. One of the best things I can share with them is the promise that they will be loved. But more importantly, I tell them that the families that we are born into sometimes aren't good families. The best decision of my life was finally leaving home. Even the dreaded unknown was preferable to the years of shame, silencing and violence that I'd endured. To this day I don't talk to my mom, and my dad has long been out of my life. My siblings are now young adults, and I hope we can eventually reconnect, but there is still a lot of healing to do.

But no matter where I've lived, I've always taken that angel with me.

14. WHAT WOULD I DO WITHOUT YOU?

RYAN FITZGIBBON | SYDNEY, AUSTRALIA TO NYC

I KEEP A LITTLE space for him. Like the memory box tucked away in the basement of my parents' house — only it comes with me everywhere I travel.

I first made room for him that night along the harbor in Rushcutters Bay, where I waited patiently for him to arrive by the second park bench from the boathouse. I had just moved to Sydney from San Francisco and was looking for friends, tour guides or really anyone I could connect with in this new city. When he greeted me with two bottles of cider, a warm hug and a cheeky smile, I knew instantly he'd be staying for a while.

That's when that little space for him was created, and in the weeks and months that followed, the access I had to it was a 24/7 arrangement. Whether we were together or apart, he had permission to consume my thoughts entirely. You never anticipate anything less in the heat of love.

You see, he provided everything I was looking for in a Sydney companion — becoming my best friend, my Australian tour guide and eventually my housemate. He opened up his life to me, and I took it all in. I allowed him to bulldoze my brain, seizing every inch of real estate so we could hurry up and begin construction on our new life together. This was our new life in Australia — where I was 10,000 miles away from my home back in the states, here on a one-year travel visa. The thrill of the unknown and the dream of new adventures together split between our respective home countries was lustful.

In hindsight, it wasn't the most sustainable or realistic approach to building a stable future together. So once we pulled our heads down from the clouds, we were finally able to see the cracks in our foundation, which quickly went from hairline to hazardous. After eight months of building a fantasy together, we decided to call it all off and go our separate ways. He would stay in Sydney, and I would start over in New York.

I really thought it would be easier to move on, especially given there was an entire hemisphere and fourteen different time zones between us, but I still had him, omnipresent in my mind. The new nonexistence of "us" weighed heavier than any newness I was experiencing in New York: the city that you love but doesn't love you back.

He was always with me, holding his weight, carrying just as much of me as I carried of him. Our friends used to joke and say that we were attached at the hip — and maybe they were right. Our conjoined limbs had worked together so effortlessly back then, back when dinner together was an assumed nightly ritual and invitations to social functions came two for the price of one. This was back before showering alone meant something was wrong and texting non-stop banter through the workday was totally acceptable.

Now the space he occupies is just a quaint little corner of my mind; it's there whenever I want to reminisce through the contents of our memories — a custom-built place exclusive for him, one with over a hundred different ways to access it. Simply typing the first letter of his name into any search field unlocks an entire timeline of memories. Damn the Internet for being so smart. Some consider this stalking, but I call it active remembering.

It's just that they make it so convenient these days. I can try to unfollow, hide and delete everything about him that comes across my screen, but in the digital world, I can never fully wash away the residue of his existence. I sometimes think there's a conspiracy of Instagram followers who rummage through my entire photo history only to "like" photos I took with him. I'm not sure who's to blame here: me for my impressive filtering and hashtagging skills, my ex for being so handsome or the rogue follower who won't let me forget it. Little reminders like this make it hard to escape him. Thanks to the Internet, the time it takes to heal wounds lasts as long as it takes to fill my archive with enough new memories, pushing him off the proverbial homepage of my life.

Entrances to this emotional minefield, foolishly mistaken for memory lane, appear in real-life everyday conversation, too. There's no better indication of my readiness to move on than how often I catch myself thinking about him in a casual conversation, making him the secret subject of everything. It's as innocent as when I met someone with his name at a party, where that insignificant fact slipped out of my mouth before even stating my own name. There was a brief pause and an awkward laugh from everyone, and I tried to save myself with and an absurd punch line about how I could think of a few nicknames if he stuck around long enough. I sealed it with a campy wink.

Another time, I misinterpreted a harmless question about what good movies I'd seen lately as a backhanded way of making me confess that I had not been to the cinema since before the breakup. Basic translation: "I'm not emotionally available to indulge in these pleasantries, so ask me how I'm doing instead. Ask me about the last movie I saw with him and how he always had to have his own tub of popcorn and how nice it was to hold his hand in the theater and when I think I'll work up the courage to see another asinine rom-com again."

Yeah, definitely not ready.

Over time, these methods of proactively keeping his memory alive occur less frequently, but I can still stumble into that space unexpectedly, as if through a series of trap doors. It's always without warning — and usually at the most random and unwelcome times. I fall into it while on a third date with a guy I meet on OKCupid. He who seemingly can do no wrong tells the waitress he "despises" Brussels sprouts and wants to substitute them for "any other seasonal side." This is before turning to me and making a face that suggests he's about to puke right there in front of me — as if he knows that Brussels sprouts were our favorite and he is testing how deep the thought of him still cuts.

I fall again on the dance floor, when I'm blissfully taking cues from Robyn's guidebook on how to be single, but then Whitney suddenly shows up and reminds me that on my own is not how I want to be dancing, but with somebody who loves — or *loved* — me. Going back to these unpredictable times feels like falling into a vortex of inescapable truths.

When he and I were "us," the memories we were building seemed unbounded and inconsequential. Now these relics are the breadcrumbs that lead me back to "then," like the shirt he let me keep because it looked better on me anyway, our secret code word for sex, the wallet he gave me for Christmas or the names we chose for our fictitious children. I don't think I will ever be able to disassociate these things from him — every time I see or hear them, I'm immediately sent back. I'm sent back to Australia, back to Rushcutters Bay on the second park bench from the boat house, back to the promise I felt from the first date and the first kiss and the first time I told him I loved him. Back to the cubby where I store all the mementos he left behind.

Some days I wish I could empty the trash and clear him from my head for good, but the reminder that "this action cannot be undone" heightens my apprehension and makes me retreat. Keeping him there means the occasional resurfacing of wounds that I know are still healing — but I have to admit, there's a comfort in the tortured recollection of what we had. It's reassurance that all the time it took to fill that space wasn't for nothing, even if the weight of it is hard to bear.

So I carry it. Everywhere I go — Bryant Park, on the train, the park bench where I sometimes eat my lunch on the East River, morning runs over the Williamsburg Bridge — he's still there, waiting.

I keep him for a number of reasons, post-rationalized perhaps. There's that sliver of hope for the fairytale ending we're promised in every Hollywood depiction of "love." It's hard to escape the temptation of those "what ifs" especially when trapped in denial. There's the hope I hold on to for the day when the thought of him doesn't make me want to vomit — or worse, grab my phone and text him to tell him that I thought of him and it made me want to vomit. Experiencing nostalgic thoughts shouldn't require a sedative. I'm getting there.

I think I keep that little space for myself — and for my own satisfaction of knowing that I meant something to someone once. I don't need to hear him say these words to know it's true. I think maybe that's the real purpose these memories serve. It's my reminder that no matter the length or complexity of the relationship we experienced, I have maybe left an impression that's just as meaningful as the one he's left with me. The space I keep for him is more than just a time capsule; it's part of the definition of who I am.

And I hope he keeps a little space for me, too.

15. GANDHI SCHOOL OF HOOKUPS

JAIME WOO | TORONTO, ONTARIO

THERE ARE A SERIES of firsts with Grindr.

The most common is obviously experiencing the hookup app for the first time. I joined in June of 2009 after learning about it from friends while having drinks on the patio, of course, and I remember the wonder and thrill of having in my hand a world of available, nearby men. It was a heady time for technology, a few years after the tipping point of Twitter and a year before Instagram, and I was intoxicated by a sense of possibility. Could the lofty promise of social media's ability to connect even spread to mobile cruising?

It's not that Toronto necessarily needed Grindr. The city is inclusive and safe, steadily more progressive over the past three decades after a bathhouse raid incited the queer community to become more activist-oriented — the Canadian equivalent of Stonewall. At the same time the app was perfectly situated, representing the future of cruising, decentralized from parks and bathhouses, for men able to travel anywhere and everywhere.

There's the first time an encounter successfully happens, which nearly makes up for the disappointments from the flakes and the missed connections. Even if the sex isn't that great — and the only ones constantly having great sex are high, lying, or very lucky — there's the novelty of summoning a man on demand. The intoxicating perfume of having sex literally at your fingertips quickly dispels, but those first few hookups are electric and sometimes endearingly awkward.

Of all the firsts, however, the one I remember best was the reaction to uploading a faceless torso to my profile. I got a reasonable number of messages when my face was in the picture, but it paled to the spike that happened once I went anonymous, the same photo but cropped to end at the hint at my jaw.

Men came out of the woodwork, and it was understandable. A profile without a head sometimes signals a readiness for action, a literal unwillingness for chatter. In addition, messaging a torso has an almost lottery-like allure: Grindr can be read as a game and scoring an anonymous user's face can act as a minor win. (Getting them in bed, naturally, is the ultimate win.)

I noted how aggressively these users would chat, sharing in detail how hot my photo was, the sex they wanted, and their fervent horniness — all to an anonymous stranger, which I imagine was part of the allure. Inevitably, they would ask for a face picture, and I would comply sending the original version of the photo, head appended. The majority of men would then vanish, either no longer responding or, less ambiguously, blocking me.

On one hand, this busted face can only get me so far. (I'll wait while you look me up on Google. Check Twitter, my photo's better there.) Another possibility, however, is that I'm of Chinese descent. I leave my ethnicity unstated on hookup apps, so when I send my face it's not so much whether it is cute or not, but that I was never an option.

It's a fool's game to attempt to figure out without doubt why men reject you on Grindr, but it doesn't stop me from wondering why race plays such a pivotal role in attraction for many. Until I had experimented with a faceless torso, I had no reference point for the volume of messages I received. Now a trend was emerging.

Growing up in multicultural Toronto, where people of colour collectively are the majority, it wasn't until my mid-twenties that I realized being Chinese was a disadvantage to my sex life. I sought out serious relationships and with so many variables at play in figuring out something long-term, I was shielded from how race could be a deal breaker.

I wasn't naive. I knew race played a factor, but I thought I was better than that and so was everyone around my age. I was wrong on both accounts, and Grindr helped hammer the point home. Repeatedly seeing a non-trivial percentage of profiles on not just Grindr but nearly all apps explicitly rejecting Asians made me confront the truth, especially when it wasn't just Toronto but Manhattan, Boston, Los Angeles, Montreal, San Francisco, and London, too.

For certain, racial tensions and assumptions aren't unique to gay culture. Evidence of stereotyping is as easily available as a short trip to the Google search engine, which will auto-complete queries with the top searches by other users. The results for race provide a glimpse into the global mindset.

Type in the words "Why are white men" and Google will helpfully complete the query with the adjectives from the top searches: "attractive," "handsome," and "weak." For black men, Google users wonder why they are so strong and attractive but also aggressive?

Why are Latino men so attractive, romantic, controlling, and jealous?

These searches are eerily congruent to the pervading stereotypes, and the tone is generally positive. It becomes less favorable for those of Asian descent. Why are Asian men so feminine, unattractive, weak, and skinny? Why are Indian men so creepy, desperate, and unattractive? The sole exception appears to be for Korean men, described as hot, cute, and tall but also rude. (No one's perfect.)

I doubt these stereotypes are shocking or novel for most people, but where is the work to counteract these? The conversation about race often feels like it is stuck in between gears, a stuttering that sounds like action but isn't. Race needs to be talked about because it still acts as an artificial barrier between people.

Even in Toronto, the dialogue can be frustrating. Actually, it can be even more frustrating in Toronto because people conflate having multiculturalism with being multicultural. The former is satisfied allotting enough space for any group that so chooses, while the latter requires not just the space but meaningful, cross-cultural interactions as well.

Race is a generally difficult conversation to have — but even more so in gay culture. A piece in the now defunct local gay scene magazine *Fab* called to attention the negative racial language used in hook-up apps, and when it went viral, the author received mostly negative comments (from Toronto and abroad) that he was either overthinking it, being too sensitive, or infringing on men's freedom to fuck whom they want. If the retorts ring familiar, it's because they are the same ones used to deflect criticism from women, visible minorities, and (yes) even queer people: this is the vernacular of the majority whose privilege is put into question.

It's probably wrong to hold Toronto — and its queer population — to a higher standard over a more homogenous city just because it is so multicultural, yet the sexual dynamics here illustrate how pervasive racial implications are in gay culture, in spite of being situated within a mixed, urbane environment.

Attempts to hold discourse on race are sometimes countered exasperatingly by the question: "Why does everything have to be about race?" Not coincidentally, I am asked this nearly every time by white boys, those who are rarely made to feel self-conscious of their skin, always the default to everyone else's so-called exoticism. They say proudly "I don't see race," but never second-guess yet another white boy on the cover of a magazine or in the throes of passion on *Sean Cody* or parading in an underwear clip on YouTube that gets passed from one to the next to the next as the gold standard for desire.

They stare at me, fatigued by their apparent need to defend their whiteness. I always assume the best in people, and trust me, I tire of pointing out the problematic, too. Especially because it opens me up to a host of criticisms: the nag, the killjoy, the spoilsport. But, then, isn't that how power structures work? It's the gentle nudge to get back into line. We're at a point where our conversation is so embryonic, some white men, shocked that they could be lumped in so anonymously, so carelessly by race, can ask: "Isn't that, like, reverse racism?"

There will be some who misinterpret this as displeasure at having fewer available sexual partners. This reading would be wrong. Instead, it's about the exhaustion that results from constantly fighting against being rendered invisible, and it doesn't get more literal than being blocked and hidden on Grindr. It is the inability to obediently accept that someone who looks like me, or more accurately, someone who comes from the same continent as myself has few venues to be seen.

It bears tangible consequences: racial perceptions in gay culture are exacerbated and further concretized by how closely linked they are to the sexual identities of men of colour. Any person with experience watching gay pornography would recognize that black men perceived as strong and aggressive often perform the role of dominant tops while Asian men, seen as weak and effeminate, are usually bottoms and submissive.

White men get a broader range of sexual roles and are rarely reduced to their race. Although this doesn't guarantee more sexual attention, it does free them from some of the prejudiced baggage that can come from automatically activated racial attitudes. In gay culture, sexual currency is by far the most privileged, likely because the mutual bond between all gay men aside from identifying as men is the desire to have sex with men, and thus being undesirable affects more than just one's relationships involving sex.

The saddest part is that the bar is already set so low. We are at a place where just the homeopathic presence of men of colour is considered a victory. It was with an arched eye that I read Tim Dean's *Unlimited Intimacy*, as he proudly contrasted the lily-whiteness of mainstream gay sex to the openness of bareback culture. I waited for Dean to scaffold his assertion with voices from people of colour, but the book remains filtered primarily through his lens; instead, he offers a trio of examples, including one where the appearance of a single African-American and "several" Asian-American tops in the film *Fucking Crazy* represents not just the "striking diversity" of the film but of the whole bareback culture.

I take it upon myself to do a search on Google for bareback porn and survey the top results, and through the dozens and dozens of models I don't see diversity being reflected nor celebrated: it remains mostly white men, some Latino and black men, and one Asian performer. I'm not suggesting that men of colour don't participate in bareback culture, but I don't believe it's proved to be welcoming by either Dean's work or representation in pornography.

While it's not necessarily problematic for a white academic to assess how race is perceived in gay culture, there's something treacly about the majority speaking to the status of the minority, especially when Dean's evidence allows a read of tokenistic cherry-picking: the word "Asian" appears only twice in the main text of his book and only in the section meant to demonstrate racial diversity. Having Dean be the arbiter for diversity then feels akin to a "Mission Accomplished" moment, unearned and edging on comical.

Of course, it's not just Dean, and it's a bit unfair to single him out; however, he serves to show how easily lip service can sweep race off the table. Race is clearly a big issue to tackle, and our prejudices run deep. I mean, if people are able to discount others based on hair colour — shoutout to all my sexy redheads — where does that leave us with skin colour?

I often think about our capacity for change. In just ten years, the majority of Americans have gone from banning to supporting same-sex marriage, a development almost impossible to believe. It was just forty years ago that homosexuality was no longer considered a mental illness.

And still, the mind appears selectively-permeable, some ideas able to be absorbed, while others rejected. Sure, in our minds we can envision two men or two women at the altar and homosexuals not in the asylum, with regards to attraction the general consensus is that men will want whom they want and what attracts them unchangeable.

This was confirmed for me last spring when I was in Boston for lunch with a man who had made a substantial fortune off the desires of gay men. I was in town to discuss hook-up apps, and over crab cakes I ventured that they could act as a vector for expanding sexual tastes. He looked at me incredulously. "Gay men can't change," he said adamantly.

You can't shift desire. This is an argument I hear repeatedly, as if it were a fundamental truth. Maybe it is like our eye colour or the size of our ears: our desires develop until they don't. It's such a comfortable idea, romantic even, this commitment to what stirs us within and then to plant it into the ground like a flag. "If I could want someone of a certain race, I would!" exclaim some, like modern day misunderstood Frankenstein's monsters, helpless in their creation. There's something seductive about assuming it to be out of one's hands.

And yet it is not a truth. What turns us on changes; desire is plastic. It has to be so to allow for statements like "I used to be into twinks and now I'm into bears." It becomes even more obvious when we concede that what is erotic, for instance, at 48 is different than at 18, as three decades of experience shape our interpretation of the world. Children favour the simple flavors of candy, while adult palates should be able to appreciate more complexity, but it takes work.

Gay men like to view themselves as sexually progressive, liberated from the outdated, close-mindedness of the mainstream. So there's an unsettling, nauseated feeling in following this logic toward its implication to race. What kind of cognitive dissonance allows gay men to relay proudly their kinkiness, their adventurousness, their readiness for pleasure without limits, but suddenly find their bounds around race and ethnicity, that skin colour and eye shape must be calculated as insurmountable?

I couldn't help but wonder if it wasn't that gay men couldn't change but didn't want to change. My lunch date, a businessman whose company grew by providing the path of least resistance, would not have been able to note the nuance. The choice many make is to dig deep into what's already known or surfaced.

To be honest, I don't blame them, and although it may appear contrary, I try not to judge them. All I attempt to do is sound the alarm that the walls are not as solid as they appear. I know desires can change because I have made it happen first-hand.

When I was younger I only dated white men and rarely considered someone of Asian descent. In the beginning, I told myself it was because I didn't feel any attraction. I certainly didn't make an effort either: in fact, all of my attention went solely to white guys. Clearly, it was just because there were so many of them, I reasoned. It was a matter of statistics.

This changed in my mid-twenties when I started to dating a man who lived in the Church-Wellesley Village, Toronto's gaybourhood. A makeup artist originally from Montreal, his place was a textbook example of design and taste, whereas I, a former engineer, tended to keep my possessions in heaps and piles. Nothing ever got lost, but there was no incentive to find stuff either. Of our two spaces, his was undoubtedly better, and it meant we spent many nights walking along the spine of the Village, Church Street, to either arrive at or leave his place.

On the street, we'd bump into many of his friends and they would stop to say hello. My boyfriend at the time would give them the customary double kiss and then make introductions if they had never met me. More than once, they would smile brightly and look me up and down, before chit-chatting with my boyfriend. I wouldn't think too much of the encounter, but apparently, my boyfriend dating an Asian would cause a stir. The next time my boyfriend would see his friend, he'd be inundated with questions around what it was like.

I was forced to confront my views on race when I began to fully understand how my own was perceived. He would roll his eyes as he shared some of the questions he got asked about me. At first he had found them amusing, but he soon got frustrated at being asked the same insipid questions.

Through these questions, it became obvious that Asian men were seen as many things, mostly negative. Was I effeminate? (No, he'd reply.) Was I a bottom? (Sometimes.) Poorly endowed? (No.) How could I grow a beard? (Actually I still get this one a lot.) I could imagine these same questions being asked if I were white, but they would be framed entirely differently.

Could my own disinterest in Asian men then have had anything to do with this negative view, I wondered. Had I succumbed to a wanton signal to dismiss men like myself? And if I had, what did that mean about the love I thought I had for myself?

I took this opportunity to reflect on my desires in earnest. I had not grown up only wanting white men. As a child, race didn't play a role in which boys I had crushes on in class. There were boys of every colour at my elementary school and I fell for so many of them. Yet as I got older and more able to act upon my desires, so began the miseducation.

On television, when the new wave of queer characters arrived, I was a teenager and invested in them deeply. I loved being able to recognize in these men as least some part of my identity on-screen. And yet, one part remained a gap: all the leads were white. Where were the Asians? There were zero of the men that Will and Jack dated. There were zero on *Dawson's Creek*. There was a total of one on *Sex and the City*, a background player, an accessory to Margaret Cho, and he didn't speak.

As I scoured the internet for porn, to watch men express their desire physically for one another, again the men were white, with an occasional black or Latino model as garnish. But like most garnishes on dishes, they could be easily ignored or picked off and tossed aside. Again, I tried to place myself in the scene, and I was mostly able to: I rationalized that maybe there were very few Asian men who went into porn and that if given the option they'd be treated equally. Looking back, it's difficult to tell if I truly believed this or if it was but one of those lies we tell ourselves to feel included.

Regardless, it was not difficult to see who filled the sexual roles in our culture and which types of men were signaled as the targets of desire. White men were available as objects of desire. They graced underwear ad campaigns. They were filmed in flattering light while out cruising in New York or Pittsburgh. They were penetrating and being penetrated in hotel rooms. The overwhelming message could be interpreted as: if you couldn't be white, then the next best thing was to be with someone white.

It wasn't to say that I couldn't objectively find people of colour attractive, but it was harder to imagine in my head, the real estate already populated with white men. It was so rare to see men of colour dating, kissing, sucking, and fucking. Of course they did it, but who was paying attention? It was clear to me that white men were the default for attraction, like some foundational rules written in a *Hitchhiker's Guide To The Glittery Galaxy*.

What hurt the most was when I confessed to myself that it wasn't just a disinterest in men of colour. For all of my upbringing to believe that skin colour didn't matter, some very negative attitudes had seeped inside. While each image alone may have been like a speck of sand, together they formed a dune that swallowed me whole, one that privileged white men. How had I been fooled to see things so simply?

I resolved that I would undo the messaging. I would change the rules. Who said that the only attractive men I saw should be the ones in the media? I began to actively seek out male models of colour. Into search engines I looked for Southeast Asian, Middle Eastern, Latino, and black men.

For the ones with fewer results I would watch everything available and with intent I watched as they fucked. It was so similar and yet so dissimilar. My eyes soaked in their faces, my hands imagined running down their bodies. I pictured their skin against my own.

But routine is formidable and resilient. At first, nothing happened. There were bodies in front of me, but I wanted none. I needed patience: how could years of imprinting be overturned in a matter of days?

I made an effort to tap into the core of desire within all of us, a reptilian urge we identify most with as teenagers. It is what gave us unexpected boners in swim class (heck, in any class), where looking at even a male mannequin could draw a swelling. I concentrated on finding these unfamiliar men desirable.

There is an echo of work here, of strain, but instead it could be seen as an exercise regimen. I was strengthening the atrophied muscles of desire, the ones that had weakened to the easiest, the most available, the simplest of images. Soon, the novelty became the engine of momentum. I was a kid who suddenly realized the candy shop spanned blocks.

There was bittersweetness in realizing the opportunities I had missed, the close-mindedness I had proudly owned. The idea appears ridiculous and absurd to rehabilitate myself watching men fuck, but what I stirred in myself was an appreciation for a wider range of beauty.

Soon, the ideas in my head became the actions I took in real-life. There were dates with men of colour. There were hookups with guys who looked kind of like me. I'm not perfect, but I'm more aware of how race plays a role in desire. I try to hold myself to actions that reflect who I want to be and the change I want to see. It is a form of fitness that requires constant maintenance, and I am all the healthier for it.

I return to the notion that it isn't whether men could change, but if they wanted to change. How many will defy physics and take a route of greater resistance? In a way, I enrolled myself into the Gandhi School Of Hookups, where if we believe race and ethnicity shouldn't be de facto barriers, then we must actively find ways to dismantle them.

I take comfort in knowing I'm not alone. For all the emphasis on those who do see race as a barrier, there are many who do not. The percentage of mixed race couples in America, while still small, is booming. Astonishingly and astoundingly, same-sex couples are leading the pack.

Obviously, there remains work to be done, but it shows that progress is happening; our media must reflect it and more gay men should allow themselves to be open to it. That includes those on Grindr: at the very least, it can count as another first.

16. PAGES FROM THE PENIS BOOK

NOAH MICHELSON | WISCONSIN

SOMETHING MUST HAVE BEEN off when my mother was pregnant with me. Or, maybe "off" isn't exactly the right word. I worry that might call to mind a tiny version of me floating in hazardous neon hormones like a fetal pig pickling in a jar at the back of a high school biology lab.

But something was different. It must have been. What else could explain why from the day I was born all I've ever been able to think about is having sex with men?

*****

The first 18 years of my life exist like a handful of moments from a not entirely terrible movie I know I once saw but now can only recall in blurry bits and pieces: a road trip to the Black Hills; a single tooth jutting through the skin just below Kiana Harding's lower lip after she fell off of the monkey bars when we were in third grade; a part of myself securely locking into place — if only for a few minutes — with a delightful thunk when I slunked off to my grandmother's bedroom and secretly clamped her faux ruby clip-on earrings onto my then tiny ears. But mostly, those years are just a long fuzzy stretch of darkness.

So it shouldn't come as a surprise that the first glimpse of my sexuality revealing itself came as a story and not a memory. My mother claims that once at a large family function, probably a birthday party or a breakfast celebrating some vaguely Christian holiday, she saw me happily masturbating. I was only three years old and she took me into another room and explained that what I was doing was totally fine but I should only do it when I was alone — not in a room full of other people unwrapping gifts they didn't want or passing a plate of soggy bacon to one another across the dining room table. She remembers I appeared to take in what she was saying and then ran off to rejoin the rest of the group. A few minutes later she noticed that I, once again, had my hands in my pants. She approached me, probably a bit befuddled as to whether or not I had really comprehended anything we had just talked about, and asked, "Noah, what did I just tell you about doing that when you're with other people?" to which I responded, "But mom! I am lonely!"

*****

I grew up in Racine, Wisconsin, in the 1980s. When most people hear "Wisconsin" they think cornfields or deer hunting, which isn't wrong...it's just not exactly right — at least as far as Racine is concerned. The city, sandwiched in between the much bigger metropolises of Milwaukee and Chicago, is more industrial than rural and is best known for being the home of Johnson's Wax, maker of Raid roach killer, Ziplock bags and Windex glass cleaner.

Poison. Preservation. Transformation. It all makes sense when I think about it now. And as beautiful as the city is with Lake Michigan sewn to its spine like a shadow, it was a rotten place to grow up queer.

*****

I have always been boy crazy. Always. I would spend hours fantasizing about the father shaving in my "Pat The Bunny" book, wishing I could rub my hand over more than just his sandpaper stubble.

Every time Mr. Rogers would come on television I would pray that just this once he would change out of more than just his shoes and cardigan and would finally fully reveal himself to me.

When I was four or five I fell in love with our garbage man. All I really remember about him now is that he had a porn star mustache and he never wore sleeves during our hot Midwestern summers. One day, determined to finally take matters into my own hands, I snuck outside when I heard his truck coming down the street and performed a burlesque-esque dance in my underwear for him in our front yard. I remember the look on his face — puzzled, not quite sickened but in no way amused — when he responded, "What are you? A little queer?"

Unfamiliar with the word and still so innocent as to assume my little number could have inspired nothing less than a reciprocation of my desire from him, I ran back into the house and proudly informed my father that the garbage man had called me a queer. My father, understandably upset, moved toward the door to chase him down and confront him but he stopped dead in his tracks and slowly turned back to me when he heard me say, "It's OK, dad. I like being a queer." Surely, I thought, this must be a good thing — maybe a bit out of the ordinary, my own meager mutation — but undeniable. Possibly even magnificent.

*****

The children in my neighborhood used to play a game called "Mermaids and Pirates." I can't recall the particular rules but I do know that, as you might guess, the boys were the pirates and the girls were the mermaids. I was always a mermaid. One day upon returning home, my older brother told my mother that I was "being a girl again." There was a matter-of-fact tone in my mother's voice when she told me, "Noah, you're not a girl... You're a little boy," but somewhere inside of her she must have been panicking. Thankfully she didn't show it and though other people often didn't know what to do with me — teachers, friends, my friends' parents — I never felt judged by my parents or my brothers – only loved. When I was five and in the hospital with a rare form of cancer my parents surprised me with the My Little Pony toy stable. A few years later they bought me a little girl Cabbage Patch doll with corn silk hair named Ivy Rose. My dream of being Madonna was not only endured but encouraged and when I was 9 years old my parents forfeited one of their Saturday nights and hundreds of dollars so I could see her *Who's That Girl?* tour.

I'm not sure if I ever fully wanted to be a girl. Aside from being interested in more typically feminine activities, I realize now that part of the reason I identified with women was because men — as far as I knew in small town Wisconsin — did not have sex with men. There were no gay men there (and if there were, they were forced to take their pick between being closeted and miserable or just plain miserable). So, if I wanted to be with a man — and boy did I ever — I needed to be a woman.

*****

I don't know exactly when during my early childhood I dreamt it up. All I know is that whenever I made a wish — on a star, on my birthday candles, when I picked up a penny from the sidewalk — I always wished for the same thing: The Penis Book.

In my mind — sadly, the only place it ever came close to existing — it was a gigantic book filled with billions and billions of pages and every man in the world would be included. On the left page would be a photo of a man dressed in whatever clothes he typically wore and on the corresponding right page — of course — would be the same man, only nude. The book was born, as so many things are, out of frustration and need. I would go to the grocery store with my mother and spy a beautiful man lifting a heavy bag of dog food into his cart and be distraught that I couldn't see him naked. If only there were some way for me to be able to see every man in the world naked whenever I wanted! I knew it wasn't technically possible, so if it were ever going to happen, it would have to be a work of magic or an act of God. If wishes were penises, oh how I would have loved to ride.

*****

Not everything was fantasy. While the only fruit my failed seduction of the garbage bore was me, not all of my advances were unsuccessful. Though, they couldn't really be called successful either. In some ways I looked at the boys in my neighborhood as prey, and in other ways, as partners in a scheme they didn't understand and weren't, for the most part, interested in. But I knew what I wanted and their confusion and indifference didn't stop me — or stop things from happening.

I have one especially clear memory of being six or seven and pretending to be Russian soldiers with a friend of mine from the neighborhood. I don't know why we chose to be Russian — maybe even then, Cold War child that I was, my queerness caused me to subconsciously identify as an enemy of America or maybe I just thought Russian guys were hot — but, regardless, there was a pup tent set up in my friend's basement and we did all of the things we imagined soldiers did around their campsite. There was marching and saluting. There were fake fires to build and feed. There were guns to clean and aim and shoot. But the thing I was most concerned with was getting my friend into the tent.

Once I did, I found ways to make things happen. But it was never enough. I was not yet an expert of the sexual arts and my friend was even more clueless and, what's more, the desire just wasn't there for him. Even though I knew what I wanted to do wasn't "right" (but pushed past that feeling for the sake of momentarily satisfying my insuppressible hunger), I don't think it had anything to do with shame for him at that age. It was just that we would only get so far before he was ready to "wake up" and see how much ground the enemy had made during the night.

*****

Sometimes I joke that for me to have had the urges I had as often and as intensely as I did as a child, my parents must have been part of a satanic cult that performed sexual rituals on me and I can't remember it because my mind has protectively blocked it all out. Or at the very least you'd think that they were heavily into porn and that I must have caught glimpses of Debbie doing Dallas (and Detroit and Duluth and...) through a keyhole. But they weren't. And I didn't. No naked pentagram parties in our basement, no spread-eagle video vixens. My brothers and I weren't even allowed to drink soda.

*****

Even when I was pretending to be a woman, I was still in love with my penis. When I was in Kindergarten I excused myself — we were busy working on some craft project with macaroni or pipe cleaners — and went to use the single-occupancy bathroom located just off to the side of the classroom. While I was peeing I began to sing a song about my penis. I don't remember the words, all I remember is that it was a sweet, celebratory little tune. A few moments later there was a knock on the door and I heard Mrs. G, my teacher, telling me that I needed to finish up. I pulled my pants back up and returned to the class thinking nothing of what had just happened but only a few seconds of silence passed before Neda Salinas blurted out, "We could hear you!" and everyone broke out laughing.

It's the first moment in my life that I remember feeling truly ashamed – and of something that up until then had brought me nothing but joy. Now, suddenly, my penis — and the things I wanted to do with it — were things to ridicule, things to shut up about — and in many ways, even at that young age, it was a certain kind of a beginning to a certain kind of an end.

*****

Like most other boys, as I approached my teenage years masturbating quickly became my favorite pastime.

Since the Internet was still years away and seeing as there were no other easy ways for me to get my hands on porn, I had to get creative. But, honestly, it really wasn't that difficult to find inspiration. Almost anything did the trick. I would get off to the line drawing of the handsome naked man with his modest erection in the sex-ed book my parents had bought for me. I would come while looking at a photo of a shirtless male ballerina featured in an old calendar I found in our basement. And then one day, a miracle occurred: I found my first International Male catalog in the mailbox.

For many gay men, just saying that name — International Male — brings back fond memories (and maybe a hard on). The catalog was half-filled with obscenely muscular men modeling puffy-sleeve pirate shirts and hot pink fishnet tank tops and half-filled with those same men in ridiculously themed (and absurdly tiny) undergarments (think camouflage mesh g-strings and high-cut bikini briefs made to look like tuxedos). It was about as close as a gay pre-teen could come to winning the jerk off lottery.

And for a few months, I was in nearly-naked hunk heaven.

Every day I would race home so that I could be the first to check the mail in hopes that there would be a new catalog. And because my father certainly wasn't in the market for a DayGlo cock sock, he had no idea that the International Males were going missing.

Normally I hid it under my mattress or at the bottom of my underwear drawer but one night I put it under my pillow as I planned to "read it" after my mother had come in to say goodnight to me. When she did, I didn't realize that a corner of the catalog was peeking out and upon seeing it, she pulled it out from beneath my head.

"What's this?" she asked before she had gotten a good look at the International Male open to my favorite page (and not coincidentally, the one with the least amount of fabric) — the jockstraps.

Horrified, I scrambled to find some plausible excuse but I knew it was useless — I had been caught.

"I need new underwear and I want some like that!" I croaked, pointing to a bright orange jockstrap without meeting my mother's eyes.

She didn't say anything more than, "Oh, OK." Then she put the catalog on my desk next to my bed, kissed me on the head and walked out the room.

Unable to catch my breath and feeling like I was going to vomit, I instantly began to cry. My secret was out! I loved men. I lusted after them. In garbage trucks. In grocery stores. In puffy-sleeve pirate shirts. And I wanted them to do wonderful and terrible things to me. And now that my mother knew, my short, strange life of incurable desire was surely over.

And then, a few seconds later, my door reopened and I saw my mother's figure framed in the doorway. She came over to the side of my bed and leaned close to my ear and said, not in a whisper, "There is nothing you could ever do to make us stop loving you. Nothing." Then she kissed my head again and walked back out of the room.

17. A SERIES OF (FORTUNATELY) UNFORTUNATE EVENTS: A CRAIGSLIST CHRONICLE

JEAN-PAUL BEVILACQUA | TORONTO, ONTARIO

IN HIS BOOK (AND my personal bible), *The Velvet Rage*, Dr. Alan Downs describes the second stage of the gay man's development as a compensation for the overwhelming shame felt while in the closet. He paints the newly out gay man's desire for casual hook-ups and brief sexual encounters as not necessarily a celebration of his sexuality, but rather as a coping mechanism for a set of "distressing emotions." At the top of that list of emotions, he states, is loneliness. He goes on to explain that, much like the monster under the bed that's not really there, our fear of loneliness is generally unfounded and not based in reality. Over five years after coming out, I can say that personally this has proven to be the case. It is through this psychoanalytic lens that I now view (and have come to understand) the following series of events that took place in the year following my coming out.

Here I was: a gay man who had recently openly and firmly declared to the world his fundamental truth for the first time. Now what? I had flirted with men in the past, lost at least part of my virginity (while still primarily in the closet), but had yet to really explore myself and my sexuality in a profound and honest way. I wondered how to go about beginning this journey.

Naturally, I turned to Craigslist.

In the days before location-based hookup/dating apps for our smartphones, there existed (and still exist) an online realm of darkness, desire and deviancy: the Craigslist "Casual Encounters" section. It was with little trepidation that, not long after my official coming out, I plunged into the depths of this wonderfully sordid corner of the internet. By "plunged," of course, I mean that I was perfectly fine engaging with the postings from a voyeuristic standpoint — happy to read through the various mating calls, especially eager to click on the ones that had the enticing "pic" label beside their descriptors, pictures that were usually dirty. However, it took a little more of self-cajoling to bring myself to actually post an ad of my own.

After a glass of chilled white wine, I tentatively conducted a mock-creation of a post, discovering that the messages I hoped to receive in response would be directed to a real email address — meaning that, were I to reply to a potential suitor, my identity would be revealed. Being the educated and stealth young man that I was, I saw the need to create a new Gmail account for my undercover sexual pursuits. And, boy, did I ever seize the opportunity to have a whole lotta fun with these e-mail addresses. Throughout my year-long tenure on Craigslist, they covered a whole spectrum, ranging from flirty (kisstheboy@gmail.com) to floozy (upforanythingintoronto@gmail.com).

Having now created and solidified my first online alias, it came the time to take the real plunge and to truly put myself out there.

First Encounter

I used to share an apartment with my younger (but not that much younger) sister.

Although she was (and continues to be) an adult, I barely felt comfortable bringing guys I had met at the bar home, let alone a complete stranger from the internet. What this meant, then, was that I was to wait for a night when my sister returned to our family home for the weekend before I could embark on my first adventure.

After making sure that I was alone for the evening, I went onto *Craigslist.com*. Now, there are two ways that one can go about to secure a hookup: you can simply go through the ads that already up and respond to them, or you can create one yourself. After perusing through others' posts (and responding to a few with my already-created online alias for the night), I decided to put up my own. I made sure that the ad was open and inviting, yet casually detached. It included my age, a qualified statement of my attractiveness ("cute, young, relatively fit undergrad") and a declaration that I was "up for anything (as long as it was safe)."

Quite quickly, I received a bunch of responses from various guys, to which I replied to a few, and went back and forth with for a couple of minutes. We went back-and-forth for a couple of minutes, and the majority of the messages contained a dick, an ass or both. I then got a message that had a chest, a quite attractive chest, and something about it hooked me. I started corresponding with this guy and seeing what his plans were for the night. After corresponding for about twenty minutes, I invited him over.

Now this is where all my "preparation" came into play. I called my best girlfriend, let her know what I was doing and asked her to call me about half an hour from when he was to arrive to make sure I was OK. We established a code language to communicate whether I was safe or in trouble or simply wanted the guy out my apartment. Thankfully I never had to use the actual emergency phrases, but I definitely used my conversations with her to wrap things up with my partner for the night. "Having to go pick up my sister from a party" became the go-to scene for her and me to play out over the phone.

The other precaution I decided to take was to hide various objects that could serve as weapons around my apartment. Besides hiding multiple knives in drawers in the kitchen and living room, my most specifically laid-out plan involved a frying pan in the cupboard under the sink in my ensuite bathroom. The plan was that, if at any point we had entered into the bedroom and I didn't want to continue with the encounter or if I felt that I was somehow in danger, I would excuse myself to the bathroom and quietly retrieve the large metal frying pan from under the sink. I guess I would then charge at him with it and hit him over the head like we were in some sort of Saturday morning cartoon.

What would I do with him after he had passed out? Not sure. Run out of the apartment and call the police? I don't know. Thankfully it never came to that point.

Once these plans had been set into motion, I changed into my laid-back-yet-put-together outfit just as my phone rang, letting me know that the guy was downstairs. My heart was racing as I got into the elevator and headed down to find my partner for the night. I wasn't sure if I was going to recognize him and if he was going to recognize me. As is always the case with these situations, you hope that the face pic bares some sort of general resemblance to the man with whom you are about to come face to face.

There is a lot going on. There's a lot of vulnerability. You want them to resemble their picture; you hope that you resemble yours. You hope that you pass the immediate test of attractiveness for them. I came down the elevator, exited the building and, thankfully, quickly found him outside the entrance. He did resemble his picture, perhaps a little bit older, but it wasn't a problem. I saw him take me in for a second; thankfully, he said out loud that I passed the test. He had brought white wine, which was nice, so we began to drink that once we had made our back to my apartment. I was surprisingly calm given the amount of new variables and elements that I was directly dealing with, and after a glass of white, we got down to business.

I wasn't expecting that this would end up being my first time bottoming. Having bottomed since then, this experience was — in more ways than one — the tip of the bottoming iceberg. I do not recommend being with a large penis for your first time. My ass hurt for days after. That being said, it was a relatively quick and easy way to jump over that hurdle in my "gay sex checklist." The rest of the encounter was pretty unremarkable, save for the big finish: it was the first time any guy had come on my face. A couple hours after he had left the apartment, I looked in the mirror and noticed that his ejaculate had dried up and created a lovely, flaky mask. I guess I didn't realize how thorough one has to be when cleaning up after such an act.

Second Encounter

It was my first fall back to school post-coming out, and while studying at the library, I decided I needed a break — well, more of a release, really. I put up an ad on Craigslist specifically listing my location as on the university campus. I got a reply from someone who was actually pretty close to where I was working. He suggested meeting in the basement of the building beside the library. I packed up my things and left to go to make the short walk to the other building. While I was heading over, I realized that the bathroom I was to meet him in had multiple stalls and, thus, other non-participants could be present. Thankfully, when I walked in, we both spotted each other immediately, recognizing our faces from the pictures we had exchanged. I suggested we head to another washroom that could afford us a bit more privacy.

I had taken a liking to studying and working with my best friend in the computer lab on the 3rd floor of the library, and I knew that there was a single washroom (that could be locked) right across from the lab. I also knew that, having just been in the lab, that there were very few people in the immediate area. With this in mind and the cute boy in tow, I led him to this washroom. I passed friends and acquaintances of mine while walking him through the library, trying very hard to act casual given the exciting and kind of dangerous nature of the circumstances.

I led him up to the 3rd floor. He ducked into the washroom first, and I followed suit. We kept it to making out and blowjobs, but at the end, he stated that he'd "really like to get me into bed." After sliding out of the

washroom separately, he gave me his number
and we said our goodbyes.

One night later that week, he stopped
over at my apartment on his way to a party.
Things got heavy pretty quickly, and I
experienced another first: having unprotected
sex. It was, as it is often described, a heat of
the moment decision. While still inside me,
he asked, "Are we supposed to be doing this?"
I replied that I didn't think we were, but he
assured me that he'd pull out before he came
— a promise he kept. We finished up.

He went off to his party, while I
proceeded to stay up most of the night
Googling HIV transmission rates, HIV
symptoms, and all other statistics,
information and analyses relating to HIV and
gay men. I sent myself off into a frenzy of
paranoia, anxiety and self-flagellation. It was
through this experience that I was directly

confronted with the shame that comes along with the expression of gay sexuality even after having come out as a gay man. It is a theme that has run throughout my sexual life. Even though I have been able to be honest with myself and others as to who I am, I still struggle with being a proud sexual being.

The morning after, I headed straight over to the sexual health clinic on campus to get myself tested and speak to a doctor. My mom called while I was in the waiting room and I relayed to her, in vague, but not really that vague, of terms of what had transpired. I talked to the doctor who, after hearing my story, assured me that while I had engaged in a high-risk activity, the actual risk that I contracted HIV after this one specific instance was actually quite low. My anxiety was alleviated for a while but never completely until I received the negative test results and hasn't really dissipated since then, no matter how safe and/or abstinent I may be. It was a real lesson in forgiving me for my perceived mistakes, while also giving me a strong indication of what life as a sexually active gay man might look like from that point forward.

Third Encounter

In the winter later that year, while in rehearsal for a musical at a theatre on campus, I embarked on my third and final Craigslist encounter. After a long and intense rehearsal process, combined with December exams and crunch time in the academic year, I needed a moment of reprieve and release. Before leaving my apartment for a night rehearsal at one of the theatres on campus, I put up an ad online looking for some company later that evening. Prior to leaving the house, I had received an eager message from an older gentleman who I assumed was in the city on business — staying at a not awful, but not terribly nice, hotel close to campus. We exchanged pictures, but he didn't send me any ones of his face; however, he described himself in great detail, which engendered some trust within me. I had let him know that I was heading to rehearsal and that I would be in touch after, with the assumption that I would be coming over to his room after finishing up.

As rehearsal was nearing its end, I arrived at a crossroads: either to go home, or take a risk and go see this faceless businessman at his hotel. I contacted him and let him know that I was on my way over. I walked over, entered the hotel lobby, got on the elevator and made my way down the long corridor towards the room number he had given me. I knocked on the door and he opened it. To say that he was

much older than he represented himself to be
(or perhaps that I had, in my mind, expected)
is an understatement. This man was, if not in
his 60s, at least in his late 50s. The first thing
he asked me, after opening the door, was:
"Am I okay?" Being the "nice" person that I
was, I said "yes" and entered his room —
although all I wanted to do was say that I was
sorry and leave. However, as a 20-year-old
newly out gay man, I didn't have the kind of
sense of self that (at 25) I now do. So I went
into the room.

At that point, I committed myself to
making this a performance: both for myself
and for him. I made the decision to enjoy
whatever was to transpire. I found myself
creating a backstory for the man facing me
and asking me what his life was like when not
in this dark hotel room. Was he from this
country? Was he married? To a woman? Did

he have kids? Did they know this is what he did on weeknights while away on business?

Part of sticking to my commitment to making the best of the situation involved me taking control, which was uncharted territory (especially within the sexual domain). I positioned myself on top. I told him what to do, where to touch and how much pressure to use. This was only possible because I was wearing the mask of performance. By creating this persona (or perhaps unleashing one that was already present within), I was able to turn this potentially awkward (and perhaps destructive) incident into a moment of power for myself. After getting off, I gathered my clothes and other belongings that I had been strewn around the room and left.

The hotel was approximately a 5-minute walk from my apartment. I was about halfway home when I looked down at my wrist for the time and noticed that the (quite expensive) watch that I had received as a birthday gift was not in its usual place. I immediately panicked but thought that it might be somewhere in my room at home. It was not. Thinking that this man had stolen my watch, I ran back to the hotel, up to the room, and pounded on the door. He groggily let me in, already having gone to bed by this point.

My instinct told me to loudly state how inexpensive and meaningless this watch was — just in case he had, in fact, stolen it. He said that he didn't know where it was and hadn't seen it on me when I came in, so I began frantically looking all over the room, my eyes darting and my hands rummaging, finally finding the watch face down under the bed. My heavy and racing heart became weightless and happy. I thanked him for the nice night, apologized for waking him up and left the room.

As I walked back home, I replayed the night's series of events (along with my previous encounters) in my head. They had taken on a surreal quality by that point. Although all had occurred relatively recently, I viewed them with both a sense detachment and nostalgia, knowing that they would make good stories but with no desire to relive them again.

The man I was five years ago was as barely a man and more a lost boy. However, sometimes I miss the reckless naiveté and sense of exploration and sexual freedom that he represented in such a pure way. Five years later, I now find myself on almost the opposite end of that spectrum: anxiety, caution and "safety" being the dominating and driving forces behind my sexual decisions. As with my mindset in other areas of my life, I am striving for a balance — balance between living for and in the moment and ensuring that I can, in fact, live past it, into the future.

18. WHEN A BULIMIC GOES ON A DIET

ZACH STAFFORD | HENDERSONVILLE, TENNESSEE

THE OTHER DAY I was going through old Facebook photos. As I poured through hundreds of pictures of me dancing in bars, on vacation, wearing lots of scarves (I realized I am a big scarf person) and cringing at snapshots that should have never been taken, I came across a photo that I had forgotten about. It was taken in the spring of 2008, right before I graduated high school. And in the photo, I am in my theater classroom. Like many young gay men, I was a theater person. Most of us are not actually all that good at

theater, but in high school theater kids are
some of the most accepting bunch, especially
if you are creative. So that's where we hide.

Anyway, the photo was taken by one of
my best friends at the time, who was the
Grace to my Will in those days. I am holding
a certificate that states I had just won "Best
Playwright" in our theater department for an
original short play I wrote. It was called
"When a Bulimic Goes on a Diet."

The play was about a young girl who
begins to diet in high school. However, when
her mother finds out, she thinks that the
dieting is really an eating disorder and
immediately sends her to an outpatient
program at the local hospital. On the first day
of the program, she sits in the waiting room
and meets a motley crew of people who all
have different forms of eating disorders. For
example, one character carries a trash can

around at all times so that he can induce vomiting anytime he thinks he's absorbed a calorie. He is bulimic.

Throughout the play, all the characters compete over who has the most severe or debilitating eating disorder. During her afternoon with the other patients, she begins to develop bulimia herself and the play ends with her vomiting while all the other characters celebrate.

It's a dark comedy.

The play was performed at my school after I won the award and received much praise. Not because it was smart, or daring, but because a high school boy wrote about bulimia and that was fascinating to everyone, because high school boys don't have bulimia

Well, that's what my teacher said.

*****

The first time I made myself throw up was at the age of fourteen.

It was a Sunday night and my father, stepmother, and dog were all in the living room watching television. I sat in my room with a carton of sugar-free chocolate ice cream and a spoon, shoveling every drip of the quickly melting ice cream down my throat.

It was Spring and the Tennessee humidity pressed onto our bodies even as the A/C worked overtime throughout the house. I was in my room eating, which had become a daily habit over the years, especially after I started dieting around age ten. This particular week I was supposed to be on a quick-fix diet that my stepmother had given me, which she had received from a girlfriend. It looked like this:

Breakfast

Black coffee
1 piece of toast
1 boiled egg

Snack

Sugar-free Jell-O packet

Lunch

1 can of tuna
¼ cup brown rice

Snack

Sugar-free Jell-O packet

Dinner

¼ cup brown rice
1 cup of steamed broccoli
16 oz chicken breast or 6 oz steak

***Only drink water or unsweetened tea or black coffee

This new diet was supposed to help me lose ten pounds in one week. I was on Day Three and starving. I had lost four pounds.

While my family sat in the living room I had scavenged the fridge, looking for something to fill me up quickly. I had recently learned that I loved the feeling of being full more than eating. Eating was actually annoying and took too much time. After a few minutes of staring into both the fridge and freezer at the same time, I settled on the ice cream that my stepmother had bought for herself. It was even low-carb and sugar free. I headed back to my room and began eating.

Once I got about halfway through the gallon, I felt my stomach begin to hurt and decided to take a break. I walked downstairs to the kitchen to put the ice cream away. When I got there my stepmother was standing in the kitchen pouring a drink into a plastic wine glass that she loved using. She had originally bought them to only be used by the pool, but they quickly became useful everywhere: in the living room, on the porch, while doing laundry and even in the car.

"Were you eating that ice cream upstairs?"

Before I could answer she grabbed the ice cream from me, inspecting how much I had eaten. "Damn, you've eaten about all of it, I see," she said. My stomach began to hurt more, but this time I think it was a mixture of shame and the aspartame that had filled my system. "Not all of it," I insisted. "There's still some left."

She lit a cigarette and smirked, "Well, I am sure you will finish it off before I even get some." Stomach pain.

I did have a problem with this — the binge eating. Ever since I was ten I remember trying wacky quick-fix diets. This was in the era when Atkins ruled the world and no one could stop talking about how they quit carbs. I would eventually fail at each of these diets and find myself in the pantry or fridge in the late hours of the night, stealing food to sneak upstairs. I would even hide the evidence in my pillowcases.

I moved slowly out of the kitchen and into the living room to join my father. He was stretched out onto one of the sofas, beer-belly pointing up toward the ceiling like a mound of dirt you'd find on a construction site. He was an ex-football star-turned-businessman, and his body had gotten fatter as his pockets did.

"Guess what your son did?" My stepmother blurted as she passed me to sit back on the couch with my father. I hadn't figured out where I was going to sit and just stood at the edge of the room staring at the

TV as I felt both their eyes now settle on me. "He ate a whole tub of ice cream in his room. Can you believe that?" She laughed.

"No," I corrected, "Only some of a tub and it was sugar free and low-carb." For some reason, I thought adding on how "healthy" it was would ease the judgment I saw rise in my father.

"Son," he shifted in his seat so he could face me in a more direct way, "Why are you eating that shit? That's for girls. If you want to lose weight, why not just go run or something? Jesus."

Stomach pain.

"If you don't like that belly, then you gotta do something about it. Don't sit in your room eating ice cream. What the hell does that do?"

I began to look at the floor. Shame overwhelmed me. My dog lay a few feet away and stared at me. I searched her face to see if she understood what everyone was saying. Right as I thought I saw something in her eye she turned over and began licking herself.

"Nothing," I responded. That was all I could say and do. Nothing.

"If I was you, especially at your age, I would be ashamed of my body, too. I know I am big now but I could lose this if I wanted to real easy. I just don't need to."

His words soaked me like spring shower.

After a few moments, I responded, "I don't feel good. I think I ate too much ice cream. I'm gonna go to bed." I could feel them both watch me as I walked away.

I remember walking up the stairs to the bathroom that I shared with my sister without really knowing what I was going to do. I remember sitting on my knees, as if I was praying to God. I remember staring into the toilet bowl for many minutes. I remember the full moon pouring in through the window shutters and serving as my only light.

I remember even more sharply how my fingers jammed down the back of my throat — searching desperately for the spot that I had heard about that will make everything you ate, everything you hated, come right back. And I remember that moment when it did all come back and how the ice cream still tasted sweet and like sugar-free chocolate. I remember feeling a sense of accomplishment. I remember lying down on the cool tile and smiling while thinking: "That's it? That's all I have to do?"

I remember as I lay on the tile, in total bliss, I could faintly hear the television and my father's laughs. I wondered if my laugh would sound like his one day when I was much older.

*****

I came out when I was sixteen. The first person I came out to was my grandmother.

She called me after school and asked if I wanted to have dinner at her house, she'd even pick me up since I didn't have a car.

My grandmother, my father's mother, was a sweet, older black woman. She went to church multiple times a week, made incredible soul food and watched the *Lifetime* channel non-stop. Her life was simple.

Ever since I was little we had some uncanny bond with one another. There were many Fridays when other kids would rather spend time with friends at sleepovers and I'd ask to stay at her house. I think it represented escape for me, or something.

As I got older I began to slowly dislike going to her house. Not because I had better things to do besides hang out with my grandmother, but because she had only one bathroom and would notice if I disappeared for too long.

On the day I came out, she arrived at my house around 4:00 PM and honked from the driveway, signaling that she was here and I better come outside now. I ran outside and popped into her car, schoolbag in hand.

"Hay, sweetie." She cooed as she pulled out of the driveway and began making her way down the road that ran parallel to the lake I grew up on.

"Hi, Jean Jean."

"How was school today? What'd ya learn?"

I never knew how to answer this question. It always seemed too overwhelming. She obviously didn't want me to truly answer this due to how impossible it would be, so I always gave the same answer: "Stuff."

We sat in silence for many minutes as her car pushed down the road. As we drove, the sun reflected off the lake and bounced around inside the car. Her gospel music hummed just louder than the motor, and she tapped her fingers on the steering wheel. Her nails were a crimson color and she wore three gold rings that looked like painted stripes across her dark, worn skin.

"Baby, you know I love you, right?"

"Of course," I replied immediately. My stomach began to turn. Whenever someone starts a sentence off like that, it never ends in a place you want it to. "Why would you ask that?" I asked scared for what her response would be.

"Do you throw up after you eat?"

My heart stopped. The light that bounced off the lake and into the car, stopped. All I could feel was the door handle, which I clinched onto as if it were going to float away if I didn't hold on. "Hold on," a voice said from the dark places in my mind. I held.

"Umm…I…I…"

"Baby, just tell me. You're not in trouble. You know I am always here for you."

Tears began to pour down my face. My throat closed up. All I could think about was the ice cream from years ago.

"I…do. I do." Tears poured harder.

Jean Jean began to cry but never took her hands off the steering wheel. The gospel music still played on.

Tell me who can move a mountain/Move out of my way

"How often?"

And when I'm in trouble/Who's right there to help me pass every test

Tears still poured down my face. My hands shook, "Every time," I sputtered, "every time I eat."

God is able/God is able

"Baby, you know I love you, right? Do you need us to get you some help?"

God is able/ and He won't fail

"I don't think I can be helped, Jean-Jean."

The car stopped at a stoplight that brought us to Gallatin Road, the main street that ran through town. Her hand reached over and grabbed mine. I stared out the window crying, shaking.

I hadn't eaten all day, my stomach growled and I felt empty.

19. STUDS ABROAD

JUSTIN HUANG | AMSTERDAM

THERE'S BLACKING OUT...AND then there's blacking out in Amsterdam.

I remember waking up on the park bench outside my hostel in the freezing cold. It's early morning, and something smells funny. I rub my nose and I feel wetness. I look at my fingers and there's semi-frozen blood on them.

I sit up and every sinew in my body strains in protest. The morning commute bustle is already beginning to sound. I yawn and the steam from my mouth looks solid enough to slice.

Instinctively I feel around for my backpack. It isn't there. Wait, it isn't there?!

I leap off the bench and frantically look around. My backpack, the backpack that just happened to contain my entire life at that point — including but not limited to my passport, my wallet, and several gorgeously rolled joints stuffed with the finest Dutch grass — is gone. I dig in my pockets and dump the damp contents onto the park bench.

10 euros
an American dime
Chapstick
a squashed but unwrapped condom
a packet of gum
many broken cigarettes (plus a handful of loose tobacco)
a cell phone

Cell phone! I snap it open and the screen flickers to life. There's one bar of battery life left.

I walk into my hostel. The same lady who checked me in three nights before is at the desk. I approach her and she looks up from her magazine.

"Backpack left gone night," my words literally trip and fall flat on the way out of my mouth. Oh man, I'm still stoned. She scrunches her face at me, and then goes back to her reading. "You checked out yesterday," she says.

End of discussion, apparently.

Back outside, I take several deep breaths of the winter chill and brace myself for the shit-eating phone call I now have to make. What time is it in California? I dial home.

A couple rings, then:

Mom (cheerful): Justin! Where in Europe are you now? Are you having fun?

Me: Hey, Mama.

Mom (instantly knows): What's wrong? You sound upset.

Me: I screwed up, I'm sor-

BEEEP! The phone dies with a sad wail of defeat.

Me (shakes fist at sky): AW SHIT!

Random Passerby (muttering to herself): Klootzak.

A hangover is beginning to sink over me like a wet blanket of regret. I need coffee. Or food. Maybe both. Definitely both. And then I will reassess.

As I walk onto the thoroughfare, shielding my eyes from the glare of dawn, I can feel more stares than usual. I realize I must still have blood on my face. My legs are cold. I look down. There's a giant tear in my jeans, right over my left thigh, which is now winking at the Dutch public as I stumble down the street. I try to pull my Oxford sweatshirt down over the gaping hole, but it's too small.

The street is really crowded now, and a noise starts to blare exponentially louder in my ears. I look around, trying to figure out what it is, when...ZOOOM! A massive tram whizzes past me, missing me by about a foot and spinning me around. I plant my foot right into an icy puddle. As I regain my composure, I hear snickers passing by me, and I know exactly what they're thinking:

Another dumb American kid gets too fucked up in Amsterdam.

*****

The funny thing is, I predicted this would happen. Or at least, I joked it would. After studying abroad at Oxford during the fall of

353

2007, the plan was always to hit up the party capitals of Europe. "And I bet you I'm gonna black out and lose my passport in Amsterdam!" Did you know that I'm a comedian?

But by the time we embarked, I had fallen in love with the city of Oxford, and it was hard to leave. Between the cobblestone streets, the gorgeous architecture, the farmers' markets and the random wells, wherever I strolled, the theme song to *Harry Potter* looped on repeat in my head.

The first night I moved into my dorm room at University College — which happened to be directly under the one that once belonged to C.S. Lewis — I explored the town by myself and wandered into a pub called The Bear that was 600 years older than the United States. As I sipped on ale, wondering why it was room temperature and flat, the barman told me about all the famous noblemen that had been assassinated there. When I joked that I should "pour one out for the homies," he cringed.

About halfway through our program, I met an Irishman named Paddy, and I swear to God that was actually his name. He went to another one of Oxford's many colleges, and he had a gleaming white smile with big teeth that were endearingly crooked.

We kept bumping into each other at local Tesco's deli section, and I didn't realize he had been hitting on me until he finally asked me out for a drink. He was the first person to ever earnestly pursue me like a gentleman, and when we finally kissed, his big teeth scraped against my lips and sent tingles down my spine. For two months we slept in each other's beds.

He was fresh on my mind as we boarded the airbus to our first destination, ironically his homeland. Our goodbye the night before had been rushed and mostly physical, neither of us daring to lend weight to what we had beyond an autumn fling.

So in Dublin I drowned my sorrows in pintfuls of Guinness. There's nothing quite like authentic, Ireland-brewed Guinness. I could've bathed in the stuff. Rich, frothy, creamy, chocolaty, soul-warming really, Lady Guinness hugged me to her bosom and made everything better. On our last night there, we went to a gay club called the Georg and I danced with fit lads and tried not to think about Paddy, and my sweat reeked of hops.

Onward we pounced upon Barcelona, where I drank absinthe for the first time (it didn't do anything) and ate paella that reminded me that wonderful food does exist outside of the United Kingdom. I ended up spending the last two nights with a local Spanish boy named Mario who had just the right amount of silky black chest hair; it was fun to pet and it tickled my cheeks at night.

The morning we were supposed to be leaving for Amsterdam, I woke up late and panicked in Mario's bedroom, until he plopped me onto the back seat of his scooter and took me to the airport. I perched precariously onto the square inch of padding that was supposed to be the passenger seat and wrapped my arms around him as the city streaked by us in colorful blurs. It was very Audrey Hepburn in *Roman Holiday*. I stared after him for a long time when he dropped me off, until his dark wavy hair was only a speck on the horizon.

At this point, the girls I had been travelling with were getting sick of my shenanigans. I'm sure I thought it was because I was drowning in musky Europeans and they were not, but in retrospect it was probably stressful that I was always disappearing into the night. After we boarded the plane at the last minute, we agreed to part ways in Amsterdam. "But not before we get really, really fucked up together," I made them promise. They rolled their eyes and agreed.

*****

I sit in a small restaurant with a half-decent view of the Amstel River, wondering why I just spent half my remaining money on breakfast. I pick at the last few crumbs of pastry, wishing there was more, and begin to defrag my memories of the past 24 hours in Amsterdam. I search my pockets again and find a brochure tucked away in my back pocket.

Van Gogh Museum. Oh, right.

I have a flashback to yesterday that feels like a fever dream: I'm walking from painting to painting in the gallery, and tears are pouring hot down my face as I watch an artist descend into madness through increasingly troubled brushstrokes. I vaguely hear one of the girls tell me it's time to go, but I just stare at his self-portrait and wonder exactly how long it takes to cut off one's own ear. Halfway through the amputation, did he have a "What the Fuck Am I Doing" moment?

I can't quite remember what happened next, except that I briefly return to reality in the worst place possible: the secret annex where Anne Frank hid from the Nazis. They actually have a recording of an actress pretending to be her playing on a loop as she reads the most depressing excerpts from her diary. If you are going to truly indulge in Amsterdam vice, only visit the Anne Frank

Museum when sober, unless you want to have a bad trip with time-traveling capability.

And after that. What happened after that?

Alcohol happens, joints happen, merry wandering happens. Our crew is getting along for the first time, maybe because it would be the last time. I vaguely remember us stumbling into a tiny museum under an old hippie's flat, where he had constructed a miniature village made entirely of crystals and naturally phosphorescent minerals. He had done so much acid in his life that the psychedelics had become a part of his system. He sprinkles glowing dust onto a crystal, his eyes twinkling at the beauty he created, as we sit in the black light. "A little bit of dust, a little bit of mineral," he chants. He calls his little underground world Electric Ladyland.

At some point after this, I part ways with the girls, right after we split a massive pot brownie. Called the "White Widow," it's frosted with white chocolate and has bitter chunks of hash in it — and that's the last I remember for a while. Evening begins to set in, and I'm vaguely aware that I am now in the seedier parts of the city because I suddenly hear the names of drugs being whispered to me by gruff voices.

Amsterdam does seedy very well. Dealers will just stroll past you and mutter what goods they have. "E... Coke... X... Hash..." They will walk right by you, and I suppose the idea is to follow them into a dark alley for the transaction.

There's only one more memory left. I find myself leaning against a wall, sipping beer from a bottle. Just chill, I tell myself, because even then I realize I've finally overdone it. It's dark now, and it's getting cold. This is the last time I remember having my backpack.

I'm staring into someone's living room, and suddenly a woman clad in black lingerie appears in the full-length window. Why is she staring at me like that? She begins to beckon at me as she teases at the strap of her bra. She has an eerie red aura about her.

Red. The realization slams into me like a tram. I'm in the Red Light District. The entire building is dotted with displays, where women of all shapes, ages, and colors are displayed like meat in a butcher shop.

And the men around me. The men walk up and down the street, their eyes darting from girl to girl, taking in this buffet. I walk slowly up the street and the square blocks of beautiful writhing women makes me think of a Broadway number, specifically "Cell Block Tango" from *Chicago*.

Leave it to a gay guy.

And the rest of the night — including the all-too-crucial part where I lose my backpack, bloody my nose, and rip open my jean crotch — is a missing chapter of my life.

*****

It is now around noon, and I walk around the city, reflecting about how badly my European joy ride has crashed. Mostly I wish I hadn't called my mom, since the phone had died in the middle of my sorrowful apology, and she probably is assuming I'm in an Italian prison and panicking accordingly.

Around this time, I suddenly think of Paddy and I realize how much I miss him. I should've called him instead, just to hear his voice. I try not to cry, and I wonder if he's at Tesco deli right now, and staring at the curry chicken baps and missing me.

Since parting from Oxford, I had been drinking and smoking more than I ever had.

I've always been a relatively tame person, and even in college I tended to be the designated driver. I think my travel mates had been surprised to see my descent into a stereotypical American slut backpacking through the Old World.

Now as I write this, I know that I was heartbroken for the first time and just didn't know it. This was a new pain, one that I hadn't ever experienced before, and I didn't recognize it for what it was. As a gay man, I'd only purely sexual WeHo encounters with other men. Paddy was my first love. I just hadn't recognized it at this point.

So instead, I think of his sweet face and the way he nibbled at everything, and I decide that this gnawing feeling must be horniness. And I note to myself that I haven't explored the gay district yet.

And that's when I get an idea. I'll do what any enterprising young gay American would do in this situation.

I'll find me a daddy.

*****

A gay bar in Amsterdam called The Cockring. A few patrons sit scattered about, but it is after lunch rush and before happy hour so it's mostly deserted. A bearish bartender wipes the counter. An older gentleman sips at a beer and reads from a book. His name is Gillis.

Enter a young man named Justin, barely 21. He's disheveled and bleary-eyed, and there are still traces of dried blood on his face, which he tried to unsuccessfully scrub away in a public bathroom. He walks to the bar and sits down, and orders the cheapest beer. He's down to the last of his money.

Gillis looks him up and down and makes a motion at the bartender, who nods knowingly. He pushes the Euros back at Justin and wordlessly points his head at the gentleman. Justin glances over, somewhat surprised. That was easy.

Justin (taking a sip): Thank you, I appreciate it.

Gillis: American?

Justin: Canadian. Do you speak English?

"Canadian" is a white lie, but one that Justin relied heavily upon while studying abroad during the Bush era.

Gillis: Yes, of course.

Justin nods and takes another gulp. He taps his feet on his stool, and looks over at Gillis again, expectantly, but the older man has returned to his book.

Justin (clears throat): I'm Justin.

Gillis (looks up again): Gillis. There's blood on your face, Justin.

Justin scrubs at his face with his hands, wincing in pain when his fingers bump against his tender nose. He does his best to look pitiful. Gillis takes the bait.

Gillis: Do you need a place to clean up? I live down the street.

Justin pauses a second, wondering if he's making the right decision. Then he nods his head, furiously.

Daddy found.

*****

Once we get to his apartment, he pours me tea and lets me wash up. I sit down on his couch and I think he's about to start the seduction process, but I can't help myself and I burst into tears. He sits next to me wordlessly for a long time — and even rubs my back awkwardly trying to comfort me — but he finally just lets me fall asleep.

I wake up early the next day, and I can hear him snoring in his bedroom. I gather myself and write him a quick note ("Thank you for your kindness, I'll never forget it"), and I quietly sneak out of his place.

Gillis lives on the top floor of an apartment complex in the gay neighborhood of Amsterdam, and as I walk down the stairs, the door of the apartment several floors beneath his opens, and a beautiful man in his 30s pops out to grab his mail. He catches sight of me, and thinking I'm doing a walk of shame, flashes a mischievous grin at me.

I smile back, but then I say, "It's not what you think, dude."

His eyes raise a bit, and he replies back, in music-to-my-ears American English, "You're a long way from home, dude."

And that's how I meet Robert, an ex-pat, who happened to work for the American Embassy in Amsterdam.

And they say God doesn't love the gays.

*****

I think back about Europe as a strange collision of woeful stupidity and life-saving serendipity. Robert pulled some strings and within a couple days I was back in the air headed to Heathrow Airport in London, a fresh passport in my new fanny pack.

But those last few days in Amsterdam were deliriously fun: Robert showed me the hidden parts of the city, like the best damn chips you'll ever eat drenched in mayo, the local parks that were beginning to be blanketed in snow, the coffee shops with the best grass. I slept in his bed, but I didn't sleep with him. For the first time in my life, I felt camaraderie with a gay man that wasn't reduced to a sexual encounter. I found a community in another part of the world that looked out for me as one of their own.

That's the thing about being gay, isn't it? It transcends race, color, gender, class, location, and age. It's a community that's bridged by more than sexual desire. Gay men from different worlds can cross paths and instantly see bits of themselves in each other.

My mother is waiting for me at the airport, having flown to London the moment she suspected something was wrong. She barely scolds me when I run into her arms, despite the fact that she knew that my irresponsible ass had landed both of us in shivering cold London.

As we wait for a flight back to California, she asks me how I managed to obtain a passport during holiday when the Embassies are closed. I wonder then if I should just tell her everything: I bounced from one swarthy European man to another until I happened to find an all-American stud that miraculously happened to work for the fucking Embassy. Also, I'm gay!

But that is a conversation for another day. I wouldn't be able to do it justice, nor be able to explain how it felt like a greater force guided me through the darker parts of ancient cities, and how I found comfort in the arms of strange men.

So I just hug her again and tell her that angels looked out for me.

EDITORS

Zach Stafford

Zach Stafford is a Tennessee writer who currently lives in Chicago. He has written for a broad range of outlets including: The Huffington Post, Salon, Glamour Magazine, Thought Catalog, Bitch Magazine, USA Today, and is a columnist at the Chicago Tribune's daily paper the RedEye.

Nico Lang

Nico Lang is the co-editor of BOYS, as well as the author of The Young People Who Traverse Dimensions While Wearing Sunglasses. Nico Lang is a contributor for Rolling Stone, L.A. Times, The Advocate,

Salon and The Huffington Post and his work has appeared in The Frisky, XOJane, The Guardian, Yahoo!, Chicago Tribune, IndieWire, Out, Thought Catalog and NPR. Lang is the former Associate Director for The Civil Rights Agenda and the co-creator of In Our Words.

CONTRIBUTORS

Joseph Erbentraut

Joseph Erbentraut is the Chicago editor of The Huffington Post. Aside from his writing with Arianna, this corn-fed, Wisconsin-bred writer's work has also been featured in the Village Voice, Windy City Times, Chicagoist, Gapers Block, ChicagoPride.com, innumerable ill-advised LiveJournal poems and at least one short-lived attempt at a "gay" novel. He lives in Chicago with his boyfriend and two cats. He is also a co-founding member of Subject to Change, a community-oriented queer DJ collective based in Chicago.

Eric Bellis

Eric Bellis is native Nebraskan, a ten year Chicago resident, a transman, and sometimes a writer. He collects horse miniatures, likes to read about astrophysics, and playing Words With Friends.

Alok Vaid-Menon

Alok Vaid-Menon is a radical queer trans/national South Asian activist and performance artist committed to building movements that resist white supremacy and imperialism. You can read more of their work at returnthegayze.tumblr.com and queerlibido.tumblr.com. They currently live and organize in New York City.

Patrick Gill

Patrick Gill is the Co-Creator of In Our Words, as well as the Co-Founder of the queer reading series All The Writers I Know. He is a poet, essayist and short story writer and is working on two novels. He also frequently performs at open mics in Chicago, including the Paper Machete. He is an alumnus of DePaul and developed LGBTQ-centered anti-bullying curricula for CPS schools. He is a semi-professional word-hustler and a burrito hunter. His mother thinks everything he is doing is a fun thing to do.

Joey Albanese

A born and raised Jersey boy, Joey Albanese writes about all of the questions, big and small, that we ask ourselves as we try and navigate (or avoid) growing up. He's been featured on Thought Catalog, Nola.com and NolaVie.com, where he writes a weekly column called Twenty(something) Questions. Feel free to send any questions his way to albanese.joey@gmail.com. However, please keep in mind that he probably does not know the answers.

R.J Aguiar

R.J. Aguiar is a writer, blogger, vlogger, and online personality best known for his work on the YouTube channels "shep689", "TheNotAdam", and "OutlandishTV". You may also know his work from Towleroad.com, NotAdamAndSteve.com, TheOutlandish.com, and Advocate.com. There's a pretty decent chance that you might just know him as the guy at every dinner party that loves to tell you more than you ever wanted to know about the particular type of wine that you're drinking.

Madison Moore

Madison Moore holds a Ph.D. in American Studies from Yale and is staff writer at

Thought Catalog. His writing has appeared in Splice Today, Art in America and Interview magazine. He is the author of How to Be Beyoncé and his new book The Theory of the Fabulous Class is forthcoming from Yale University Press. madison lives in Brooklyn and Richmond, VA.

Buck Angel

As an icon of popular culture, Buck Angel's passionate message of empowerment through self-acceptance and being sexually comfortable in your own skin has struck a profound chord with people all over the world. In live appearances that include YALE University and IdeaCity Toronto, Buck encourages people to think outside the box as he re-defines gender and expands perspectives on sexuality. His unconventional core concept is expressed by the phrase he coined: "It's not what's between your legs that defines you!" It has proved to be a remarkable insight and validation for men, women, and those who identify as neither, both, or other.

Jaime Woo

Jaime Woo is a cultural critic and the author of "Meet Grindr: How One App Changed The Way We Connect." His work focuses on the intersection of technology and culture. He lives in Toronto.

Shawn Binder

Shawn Binder is a finishing up his senior year at Florida State University where he is studying Editing, Writing, and Media as well as International Affairs. When he isn't writing about his feelings, he is watching Hitchcock films and hanging out with his dog.

His debut, Everything Is Embarrassing is coming out 2014 with Thought Catalog.

Mar Curran

Mar Curran is a trans*/queer writer in Chicago. They write for In Our Words, produce All The Writers I Know and Word Is Out, and perform their own spoken word and nonfiction around the city. A graduate of Loyola University Chicago with a B.A. in Communication and Women's & Gender Studies, Curran uses the pronouns they or he, and identifies as more of a cat person than a dog person. They can also be found focusing on community organizing, mainly with their fundraising/dance party collective Subject To Change every first Tuesday at Township for 18+ queers and allies.

Oscar Raymundo

Oscar Raymundo is a weekly columnist for The San Francisco Examiner. He's currently at work on a futuristic gay love novel, Confessions of a Boy Toy.

Randall Jenson

Randall Jenson is the Executive Director of SocialScope Productions, the award-winning LGBTQ documentary media non-profit. He created the 50Faggots series, which documents the lives of self-identified effeminate gay men in the U.S. In May 2013, Randall accepted the position as LGBTQ Youth Advocate at Safe Connections in St. Louis, Missouri.

Noah Michelson

Noah Michelson is the Editor of Gay Voices at The Huffington Post. He received his MFA in Poetry from New York University and his poems have been featured in The New Republic, The Best American Erotic Poetry from 1800 to the Present, and other publications. Before joining The Huffington Post, Noah served as Senior Editor at Out magazine and he has also contributed to Details and Blackbook and served as a commentator for the BBC, Current TV, Fuse, Sirius XM and HuffPost Live.

Jean-Paul Bevilacqua

Jean-Paul received his Honours Bachelor of Arts in Drama and Semiotics from the University of Toronto, and is currently in his second year at Osgoode Hall Law School in Toronto. In addition to his artistic and academic pursuits, Jean-Paul was an original cast member for four seasons on the hugely successful MTV Canada and Logo TV talk show 1 Girl 5 Gays.

Ryan Fitzgibbon

Ryan is the founder and creative director of Hello Mr., a magazine about men who date men. Prior to launching the first issue in Australia, he was a communication designer for the global design consultancy, IDEO, calling San Francisco home when he wasn't traveling across the US, Singapore, Brazil, India, or Italy for work. He now lives in Brooklyn, NY where he publishes the magazine independently.

Justin Huang

Justin Huang is a 26-year-old film producer born and raised in California. In his spare time, he enjoys semi-rigorous exercise, grilling outdoors, drinking IPA, and talking to his mother. He currently resides in Los Angeles with a puppy named Frank.

CPSIA information can be obtained at www.ICGtesting.com
Printed in the USA
LVOW12s1030270214

375407LV00009B/92/P

9 781629 213712